DAY HIKING KINGS CANYON

by
Steve Sorensen

Manzanita Press
PO Box 720
Three Rivers, CA 93271
209-561-4666

GRANT GROVE

REDWOOD MOUNTAIN

JENNIE LAKES WILDERNESS

WARNING and DISCLAIMER

Every effort has been made to provide the most accurate maps and information for this guidebook. However, as with any outdoor sport, hiking in the mountains has a potential for injury. The author and publisher of this guidebook accept no responsibility for bodily injury or loss of property by hikers using this guidebook. Hikers must exercise caution and common sense at all times.

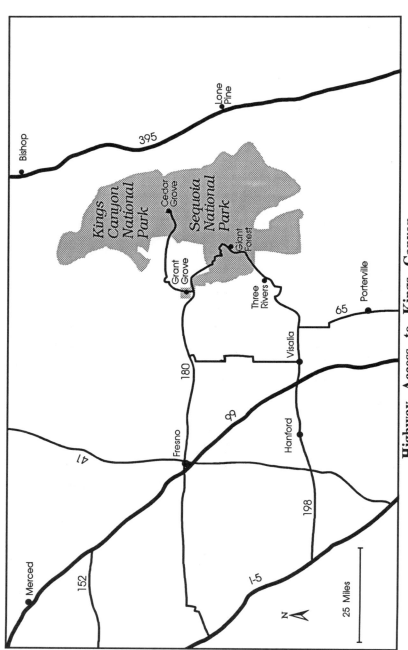

Highway Access to Kings Canyon

INTRODUCING
KINGS CANYON COUNTRY

The Kings Canyon country is a strikingly rugged country, characterized by steep cliffs of granite and marble, gnarled canyons, and raging rivers. At its heart is the massive Kings Canyon itself; if measured from the top of Spanish Mountain, to the bed of the Kings River, it is the deepest canyon in North America—nearly 8,000 feet deep. And if you measure the total uninterrupted fall of the Kings River, from the top of North Palisade Peak, at 14,242 feet, to the Pine Flat Reservoir, then the upper Kings River has the greatest vertical drop of any undammed river in the United States — 13,291 feet.

But in spite of these rugged qualities, the Kings Canyon country includes many fragile meadows, quiet streams, and virgin forests. It also includes some of the finest stands of giant sequoias in the world.

Looking at a map of Kings Canyon, you see that most of the area within the boundaries of Kings Canyon National Park is not accessible by road. In fact, about 87 percent of Sequoia and Kings Canyon National Parks was officially designated as wilderness by Congress in the California Wilderness Act of 1984. Together with the Monarch Wilderness, Jennie Lakes Wilderness, John Muir Wilderness, Golden Trout Wilderness, Ansel Adams Wilderness, Yosemite Wilderness, and several smaller wilderness areas, this region of the southern Sierra Nevada makes up one of the largest contiguous blocks of wilderness in the United States.

A BRIEF HISTORY

The Kings River was discovered on January 5, 1805, by the Spanish explorer Gabriel Moraga. On the following day, January 6, it was named "Rio de los Santos Reyes," or River of the Holy Kings. January 6 is celebrated by Catholics as the day the three holy kings brought gifts to the infant Jesus.

Yokuts and Monache Indians had permanent villages along the length of the river, and they made seasonal migrations into the high country. The lower Indian villages were periodically raided for Christian converts by the Spanish missionaries living along the coast of central California. Forced to return with the priests to the missions, most of the Indians ran away again at the first opportunity. As one priest from the San Miguel Mission mourned, "It is the painful experience of the missionaries that such christians, very much attached to their Tulare homes, leave the mission, and in consequence lose the Holy Mass and offend God, and hide in the Tulares region where they cannot be taken without peril and without troops."

By the middle part of the 19th Century, it no longer mattered whether the Indians ran away or not. Large numbers of them began to die, victims of smallpox, tuberculosis, and other European diseases they had no resistance to. Within a few short years there were almost no Indian inhabitants making annual migrations into the upper Kings Canyon country.

During the 1880s and 1890s a great deal of logging began to take place in the giant sequoia groves west and north of what is now Grant Grove. Logging on a much smaller scale began to take place on Redwood Mountain. Many of these old logging sites—the Smith Comstock Mill, Converse Basin, Barton's Post Camp—can be reached by trails described in this guidebook. Though their history is interesting, their effect on the landscape was massive, and devastating. In Converse

Basin, then the largest stand of giant sequoias in the world, 5,000 acres were clearcut. In many ways, it was the public's outrage over the waste and destruction caused by the logging operations in Kings Canyon that led to the establishment of Sequoia and General Grant National Parks.

HOW TO USE THIS GUIDEBOOK

At the beginning of each trail description you find the distance for the hike. This distance is one-way. Unless the hike is a loop, you must double that mileage to arrive at the total distance hiked.

Also at the beginning of each trail description is an estimated time to complete the hike. This, too, is one-way. These estimates are quite generous, and allow for time to rest, to enjoy the sights, or to simply dawdle along. Each trail description shows the starting elevation, the highest elevation, and/or the lowest elevation. Studying these elevations beforehand will allow you to arrive at your own estimate of how difficult each trail will be.

Each trail is rated for difficulty: Easy, Moderate, and Strenuous. A few are rated as Moderately-Strenuous. Of course these are subjective judgments, and not all hikers will agree with the rating for any particular trail.

Although each hike in this guidebook has an accurate and updated topographic map to accompany it, the correct United States Geological Survey (USGS) map is also indicated for each hike. It is optional to buy the USGS maps, but if you do buy them keep in mind that while the topographic detail on those maps is generally very accurate, they have not been updated since the 1950s, with some limited revisions in 1967. Several of the trails shown on those maps are no longer in existence, and new trails have been added. If you do choose to buy the USGS maps, there are five quadrangles required for all the trails in this guidebook: Giant Forest, Marion Peak,

Tehipite Dome, Triple Divide, and Patterson Mountain. There is also available a USGS topographic map for all of Sequoia and Kings Canyon National Parks, but its scale is not always useful for day hiking.

The scale on the maps drawn in this guidebook varies from map to map, which is why each map has a bar that represents approximately 1/2 mile. On all the maps the contour interval is 200 feet, meaning that each time you cross one of the topographic lines you have ascended or descended 200 feet. With a little practice, novice hikers will be able to study the topo lines and visualize the lay of the land.

At the entrance stations to the park, visitors are given a map of Sequoia and Kings Canyon. Be sure to keep that map. While its scale is not suitable for hiking, it will be your best guide for finding your way around the roads of Sequoia and Kings Canyon, and for finding the trailheads.

Every trail described in this guidebook was hiked by the author in the fall of 1991. At that time every effort was made to record the most accurate and up-to-date information available. Obviously, though, conditions will change. If you would like to contribute information or suggestions for future editions of this guidebook, write the author at: Manzanita Press, PO Box 720, Three Rivers, CA 93271.

A FEW PRECAUTIONS TO KEEP IN MIND WHILE HIKING IN KINGS CANYON

The terrain of the Sierra Nevada is as rugged as any mountain range on earth. With few exceptions the landscape is steep and rocky, and even on well-maintained trails hikers must spend considerable effort getting from one point to another.

Besides the rugged terrain, you are coping with the high altitude, which is draining your body of perhaps one fourth of its efficiency. The remedy for both rough terrain, and high altitude, is simply to go a little slower. For most hikers it will take years to see all of the trails in just the front country of Sequoia and Kings Canyon, so enjoy them slowly, one at a time.

In terms of climate, the Sierra Nevada is one of the gentlest mountain ranges on earth. Still, even in the summer the weather can change quickly. A morning that starts out warm and sunny can be cold and snowy by afternoon. Therefore, each member of your party should have a warm jacket or sweater, and at least some rain protection. You should also have matches or lighter, a small first-aid kit, and above all, a water bottle.

Hikers in the southern Sierra have been injured and killed by lightning. In most cases the hikers failed to take simple precautions to protect themselves. If any of the following conditions are present, find cover immediately: dark clouds nearby, lightning, hail, rain, hissing in the air, or static electricity in the hair or fingertips. Lightning-struck trees can shatter or even explode. Large overhanging boulders often provide the best shelter.

If you are hiking below 5,000 feet, there's a good chance you will see poison oak. In most places it has been pruned away from the trail. But if you aren't familiar with this troublesome plant, look for a shrub with shiny leaves in groups of three, and white berries. If you should develop a rash shortly after a hike, be sure to wash your clothes in hot water before wearing them again, and wash your skin with soap and hot water. There is really very little else you can do for poison-oak rash, except wait for the rash to go away. A hot shower may help relieve the itching.

If you are hiking in the lower elevations, you could encounter ticks, particularly in brushy areas, and particularly during the rainy season when ticks are more numerous. Stay on the trails, and avoid contact with brush, if possible. If you are hiking with someone else, periodically check each other's hair, neck, arms, and clothing. (If you have never seen a tick, they are brown or black, and about the size of a pinhead.) Pay careful attention to any itching on your skin; usually you can feel a tick trying to burrow into your skin before it becomes fully attached. If a tick does become attached, do not put anything on its body such as alcohol or a hot match. Carefully remove the tick with a pair of tweezers, grasping it as closely to your skin as possible. Do not try to remove the tick with your fingers—you'll only mash its body, leaving the head embedded in your skin.

You could come across black bears on any trail in Kings Canyon. Black bears are not as dangerous as their cousins, the grizzlies, which have not been found in California since the 1920s. The only real dangers with black bears are if you are feeding them, or if you should accidentally come between a mother and its cubs. If you see an adult bear, look around for any cubs, and keep your distance from them. If a bear is making a persistent effort to get food from you, shout, make loud noises, and throw small rocks toward it. Most black bears can be easily chased away.

Almost every year someone drowns in one of this area's many rivers or creeks. Often these victims were diving from the cliffs, swimming in rapids, or otherwise taking risks a cautious person would not take. But there is also the danger of the uninformed visitor misjudging the swiftness of the current, the steepness of the rocky banks, or the coldness of the water. Remember that any time you are near a river or creek there is a potential danger.

Rattlesnakes are seen most often in areas below 8,000 feet. Though rattlesnake bites aren't nearly as common, nor as dangerous, as many people think (far more people in the United States die of bee stings every year than snakebites) it's still wise to watch for them at all times. Rattlesnakes can't tolerate intense sunlight for more than a few minutes, and they become quite sluggish in cool temperatures. For these reasons, rattlesnakes are most often seen in the evening, after sunset. If you are in the foothills, be particularly alert for rattlesnakes at that time of day.

Most snakebites occur because the victim was teasing, touching, or trying to kill the snake. Your best precaution with rattlesnakes is to leave them alone. In the unlikely event that you are bitten by a snake, keep in mind that in a very high percentage of cases venom is not injected by the snake. Even if venom is injected, rattlesnake bites on the extremities are rarely fatal. So there is no reason to panic. As with any injury, remain calm and seek help from the nearest rangers.

Although the water in the rivers and creeks certainly appears to be clear and inviting to a thirsty hiker, you should not drink it. All surface water should be considered contaminated with Giardia, a microscopic parasite which can cause diarrhea and other intestinal problems. Water filters are available at backpacking stores, but their usefulness in filtering Giardia cysts is uncertain. Boiling the water is very effective in killing the cysts, though not very practical for day hikers. The best solution is to carry a water bottle or canteen with water from the campgrounds, or from some other treated water source.

It's easy to underestimate the amount of water you will need to carry on a day hike. The Sierra Nevada is often cool in the summer, but the air is also very dry. You are working hard while hiking, and it's possible to become dehydrated. For a four-hour hike, you should carry at least two quarts of water per person. Another good rule of thumb for hikers is that you should drink enough water so that you are urinating frequently, and your urine should be clear.

Every time you start out on a hike, it's a good idea to pause for a moment and think, Where is the nearest telephone, where is the nearest ranger station, and where would I go for help if an emergency did occur? From any telephone in the park you can dial 911 to report an emergency; no coin is necessary. The Park Service has several paramedics who can respond quickly to nearly any location described in this text.

Finally, some hikers may wonder how the regulations in a U.S. Forest Service wilderness area differ from those in the Park Service: Neither area allows motorized vehicles, bicycles, or motorized equipment on their trails. In Forest Service wilderness areas, however, you are allowed to have dogs and guns. Neither dogs nor guns are allowed on Park Service trails. Neither area requires wilderness permits for day hiking.

Happy Trails!

Maps Legend

Highway

Road

Featured Trail

Other Trail

River or Creek

Lake

Meadow

Trailhead

Campground

Ranger Station

Entrance Station

North Symbol

Peak

Building

Giant Sequoia

Maps Legend

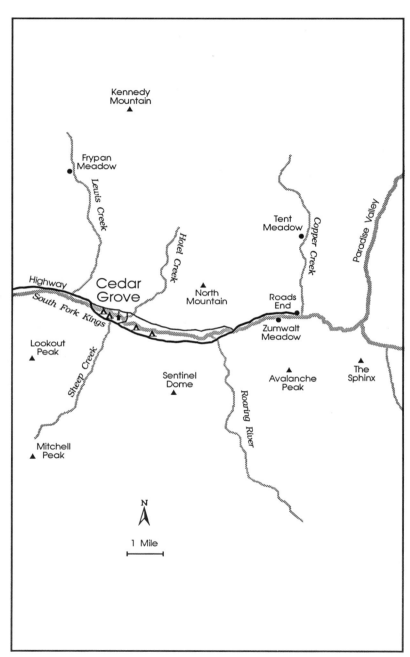

Cedar   Grove

INTRODUCTION

TO

CEDAR GROVE

From a hiker's point of view, Cedar Grove is like the hub of a giant wheel. There are trails going in every direction except down. It is perhaps best known as a starting point for backpackers heading into the vast backcountry of Kings Canyon, but there are exceptional opportunities here for day hikers as well: the Paradise Valley Trail is one of the most beautiful short hikes in California; the Zumwalt Meadow Loop, besides being beautiful, is easy enough that young children can complete it; and the River Trail is always a favorite with fishermen.

If day hikers have any complaints about Cedar Grove, it's that the place is geographically at the bottom of things. To hike very far in any one direction means you have to climb. This situation is eased considerably by the fine condition of most of the trails in Cedar Grove; with few exceptions you will find them well engineered, with a moderate grade, and almost perfectly maintained. Also, you will find that because of Cedar Grove's relatively low elevation (only 4635 feet at the ranger station), the physical exertion of climbing here isn't nearly as taxing as it is, say, at Mineral King, or even Grant Grove.

Because of the fairly low elevation, Cedar Grove tends to be warmer than many places in the southern Sierra. The summer (and even fall) nights are mild and pleasant, but summer midday temperatures often hover around 100 degrees. Canyon breezes are common, and this makes the heat more tolerable. But it is still best to get an early start while hiking in Cedar Grove. Plan on spending the middle part of the day resting someplace in the shade.

By far the greatest danger in Cedar Grove is the river. Visitors repeatedly underestimate its power, and its numbing cold. Always use extreme caution when hiking near the river, particularly if you have children.

The second greatest danger in Cedar Grove is the steep terrain, especially along the slippery edges of the creeks and the river. Despite several warning signs, many people have fallen to their death above Mist Falls.

Yet no reasonable, cautious person has any reason to fear the river or the steep terrain in Cedar Grove. Just make sure you are in the category of a reasonable and cautious person.

A few words about history: If events had worked out a bit differently, Cedar Grove might easily have become one of two things: It might have become one of the largest lakes in California. Or, it might have become a second Yosemite—that is to say, a sacred temple converted into a parking garage.

As early as 1920 the City of Los Angeles proposed a plan to build a dam at Cedar Grove, and to develop an elaborate water-control and power-generation complex on the Kings River. To counteract those interests, businessmen in the San Joaquin Valley proposed turning Cedar Grove into a major resort and tourist attraction. As usual, the U.S. Congress couldn't decide which plan to support, and therefore chose inaction.

Even after Kings Canyon National Park was established, in 1940, Cedar Grove was excluded from the park, due to the controversy over how it should be developed.

To further complicate matters, residents on the east side of the Sierra Nevada wanted to see a highway completed through Cedar Grove, up Bubbs Creek, over Kearsarge Pass, and into the Owens Valley.

It wasn't until 1965 that arguments over the future development of Cedar Grove were put to rest. At that time Cedar Grove became part of Kings Canyon National Park.

Under the master plan for Cedar Grove, completed in 1976, the valley is to remain essentially as it is today.

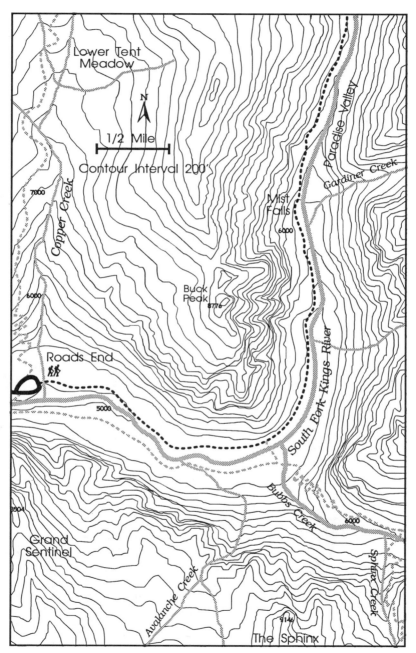

Paradise   Valley   Trail

PARADISE VALLEY TRAIL

DISTANCE: 4 Miles to Mist Falls; 6 Miles to
Paradise Valley

HIKING TIME: 2 Hours to Mist Falls; 4 Hours to
Paradise Valley

STARTING ELEVATION: 5035'

HIGHEST ELEVATION: 5663' at Mist Falls;
6586' at Paradise Valley

DIFFICULTY: Moderate to Mist Falls; Strenuous
to Paradise Valley

USGS MAP: Marion Peak

The massive power of the Kings River is a spectacle every
hiker should experience at least once in his life, and the Paradise
Valley Trail is a great place to do it. You can hike to Mist Falls,
one of the most impressive falls in the southern Sierra, or you
can continue on to Paradise Valley, which John Muir said rivals
Yosemite in beauty and grandeur

Look for the trailhead at the east end of the parking area at
Roads End, 5.6 miles from the Cedar Grove Ranger Station. At
the trailhead there's an information booth manned by a park
service employee.

The trail begins by crossing several small forks of Copper
Creek. This area was once the site of a large Indian village; a
sharp eye can still find flakes of black obsidian used by the
Indians for making arrowheads, knives and scrapers.

The site of the old Kanawyers Store is just east of Copper
Creek, and north of the trail. Peter Apoleon Kanawyer, known
as "Pole" to his friends, was a prospector who filed a mining
claim for copper ore near here in 1800s. The site became a
popular stopping point and supply station for cattleman, sheepherders and prospectors traveling in and out of the mountains,

and Kanawyer, with the help of his wife, Viola, converted the mining camp into a store. John Muir once said he would walk the length of the Sierra for one of Mrs. Kanawyer's pies. The Kanawyers Store was torn down about 1927, but at the Cedar Grove Ranger Station you can see an interesting photograph of the store when it was in its prime.

For the next mile or so, the trail passes through a broad, flat, sandy area, with only a few scattered cedars and ponderosa pines. Here and there are house-size boulders that have tumbled down from the steep cliffs above. Looking to the south you have a fine view of Grand Sentinel, which rises 3500 feet above the valley floor.

You may notice the bright green dwarf mistletoe on the pines and cedars along here. Much of Cedar Grove is badly infested with this parasite, which survives by tapping into the flesh of the parent tree and stealing nourishment. Though the mistletoe is native to this area, the Park Service is concerned that the infestation has somehow been made worse by man's use of this valley. The campgrounds at Cedar Grove are losing conifers at an alarming rate—to bark beetles, soil compaction, axe and vehicle damage, as well as dwarf mistletoe. For this reason, the Park Service is trying to eradicate dwarf mistletoe in the campgrounds at Cedar Grove. Park Service tree climbers take on the tedious, and often dangerous, job of climbing each tree to trim off the infected branches.

After the first mile you enter a swampy area, as the trail passes closer to the river. This is a good place to watch for wildlife, particularly deer and bear.

At 2 miles, elevation 5098 feet, you come to a trail junction. The Paradise Valley Trail turns to the north, uphill. If you like, you can continue on the lower trail for just 200 feet to the Bailey Bridge, where you have a fine view looking up the South Fork of the Kings. (Actually, the name "Bailey" describes a type of prefabricated steel bridge, which is why there are bridges with that name all over the country.)

If you are ready to return to Roads End, you can make a loop hike by using the Sentinel Trail, described in the next chapter.

Now the trail to Mist Falls begins climbing more steeply, staying close to the South Fork of the Kings, and passing alternately between densely-shaded groves and rocky clearings. The is one of the prettiest sections of trail you will see in Kings Canyon. There are opportunities for fishing and swimming along the way, but use extreme caution on the slippery rocks, particularly when the water level is high.

You pass through a great variety of trees, among them: ponderosa pines, jeffrey pines, sugarpines, cedars, white firs, black oaks and golden oaks.

Looking to the east, across the canyon, you can see a long, graceful waterfall on Gardiner Creek.

Looking back to the south you have occasional views of the Sphinx, the oddly-shaped rock formation on the south side of Kings Canyon. The Sphinx was named by John Muir in 1891, apparently because of its similarity to the Great Sphinx of Egypt. Muir was in the habit of naming almost everything he saw in the Sierra; some of the names stuck, others didn't.

At 4 miles, elevation 5663 feet, you arrive at Mist Falls. This is one of the most spectacular falls in the southern Sierra. There are several good viewpoints below and above the falls, but use extreme caution here. Many hikers have been killed by slipping into the river and being swept over the falls. Avoid the slippery rocks, and keep children under control here at all times.

Looking back to the south, you now have an even better view of the Sphinx and its polished granite avalanche chutes, and of Palmer Mountain, 11,250 feet high.

The trail continues climbing, more steeply now, gaining nearly a thousand feet in the next two miles. On the rocky slopes above the trail, you see occasional pinyon pines, with their twisted shapes and bluish-green needles. Fairly rare on the western slope of the Sierra, these pines are quite common on the eastern Sierra and over much of the Great Basin. Pinyon pines were highly prized by the Indians for their nuts, which are sweet and nourishing.

After two miles of steady climbing, you reach the mouth of Paradise Valley, elevation 6586 feet. Here the trail becomes nearly level. Compared to the steep and narrow canyons below, the broad meadows and gently-flowing river of Paradise Valley seem much more inviting to the human eye. The trail continues up Paradise Valley to Woods Creek, and eventually to the John Muir Trail. A very popular backpacking route, known as the Rae Lakes Loop, continues over Glen Pass and back to Cedar Grove.

You may explore Paradise Valley for a far as you like (the valley is about 4 miles long), but after their morning exercise most hikers are content to lounge along the river and enjoy the beauty of paradise.

On your return route, you can make a partial loop of this hike by taking the Sentinel Trail, described in the next chapter.

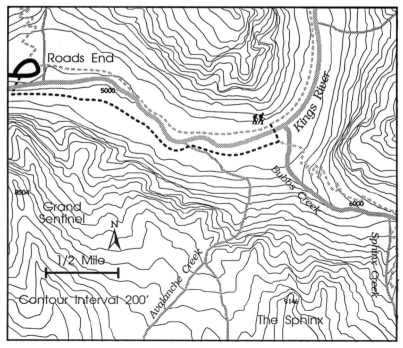

Sentinel Trail

SENTINEL TRAIL

DISTANCE: 2 3/4 Miles

HIKING TIME: 1 Hour

STARTING ELEVATION: 5098′ at the Bailey Bridge

LOWEST ELEVATION: 5035′ at Roads End

DIFFICULTY: Easy

USGS MAP: Marion Peak

This trail is really an auxiliary to the Mist Falls and Bubbs Creek trails, since its major purpose is to offer an alternate route back to Roads End from the Bailey Bridge. Even though it is traveled much less than the route on the north side of the river, it is more scenic, and offers some opportunities for the fisherman.

About 2 miles east of Roads End, the Mist Falls Trail and the Bubbs Creek Trail separate. From that junction, turn east and cross the Bailey Bridge. Continue hiking through the cedar thicket, and in less than 1/4 mile you come to a trail sign which reads, " Roads End 2.6 miles." Turn west.

You are now on the south side of the Kings River, hiking west.

The trail passes through dense groves of pines and cedars, giving occasional views of the Grand Sentinel. In the spring, this area is sometimes marshy, and the trail indistinct, so watch carefully.

After a total of 3/4 miles, you cross Avalanche Creek, which at times overflows into several smaller streams.

At 1 1/2 miles you emerge from the dense forest to an open meadow-like clearing, surrounded by ponderosa and jeffrey pines.

The ground cover here is a fine sedge, known as Carex exerta. At higher elevations in the Sierra Nevada it is the most common plant found. The tiny seeds of this sedge are very nutritious for livestock, and during the 1800s sheepherders and cattlemen drove their herds into the high country every summer in search of this plant. At this low elevation, however, and at this dry site, it occurs only in clumps.

You now cross over a low hill, or moraine, which is made up of debris left by a glacier advancing down the valley. On the south side of the trail, you see a huge boulder which provides good shelter in a thundershower.

The trail now follows the river more closely. At about 2 miles, looking north across the river, you can see a very large boulder, about the size of a house, along the river's edge. That boulder is known as Muir's Pulpit, and a good swimming hole is found at its base. For a description of a short trail to that site, see the next chapter.

At 2 1/4 miles you reach a footbridge. Cross over to the north side of the river, and follow the trail sign back to Roads End.

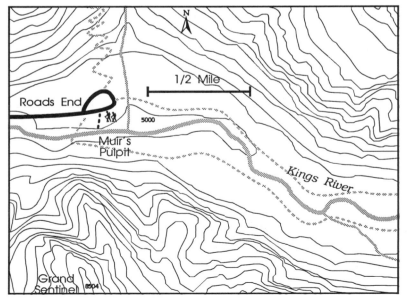

Muir's   Pulpit

MUIR'S PULPIT

DISTANCE: 100 Yards

HIKING TIME: 1 Minute

STARTING ELEVATION: 5035´

HIGHEST ELEVATION: 5035´

DIFFICULTY: Easy

USGS MAP: Marion Peak

This brief trail is included here as a fun way to end some of the other hikes out of Roads End. If you've come down the Copper Creek Trail, or crossed the sand flats from Bubbs Creek on a hot summer day, you're probably ready for a dip in the river.

Some hiker's will recognize this spot by the name of "Party Rock." That unfortunate name makes this sound like the kind of place where people go to drink cheap wine until they pass out in the sun. It isn't.

There is some evidence that John Muir held lectures on this rock, and that evidence has inspired the preferred name of "Muir's Pulpit."

The trail to Muir's Pulpit begins at the Roads End parking area, 5.6 miles from the Cedar Grove Ranger Station. As you first pull into the parking area, on your right you see a large, brown trail sign which reads, "Zumwalt Meadow...etc." Just a few hundred feet east of that sign, you see an unmarked footpath which leads south, toward the river. From the parking lot, if you look carefully through the trees, you can see the top of Muir's Pulpit, which is a large, flat-topped, granite boulder beside the river.

The boulder itself is a good place to sit and enjoy the striking view of the river, and of the Grand Sentinel. Below the rock are deep, clear pools.

Keep in mind that the river can be cold and swift, particularly in the spring and early summer when the water level is high. Use extreme caution here, especially if you have children.

Also keep in mind that diving into the river is extremely dangerous; there have been countless injuries and fatalities in Sequoia and Kings Canyon National Parks as a result of this foolish practice.

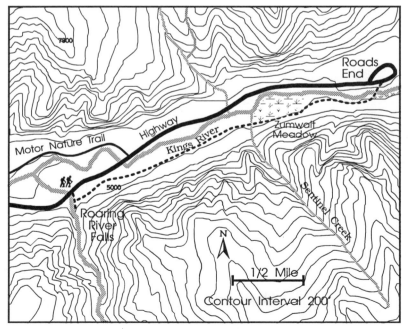

River Trail

RIVER TRAIL

Roaring River Falls to Zumwalt Meadow and Roads End

DISTANCE: 1/4 Mile to the Falls; 1 1/2 Miles to Zumwalt Meadow; 2 3/4 Miles to Roads End

HIKING TIME: 10 Minutes to the Falls; 1 Hour to Zumwalt Meadow; 2 Hours to Roads End

STARTING ELEVATION: 4880´ at Roaring River Falls

HIGHEST ELEVATION: 5035´ at Roads End

DIFFICULTY: Easy

USGS MAP: Marion Peak

This trail is the best way to get to know the plants, animals, and varied landscapes on the floor of Kings Canyon. It's route is gentle enough that anybody, young or old, fit or fat, should be able to amble over its three miles in an easy morning. To make the hike even easier, you can hike only as far as Zumwalt Meadow if you like.

Since this is not a loop hike, there is the problem of getting back to your car at the trailhead. If you are hiking in a group, after the hike you can send your most energetic hiker back for the car while the others wait at Roads End; or, perhaps the best solution is to have a driver drop you off at the trailhead, then meet you at Roads Ends for lunch.

To find the trailhead from the Cedar Grove Ranger Station, drive east on the highway 3.1 miles to the Roaring River Falls parking area, which is just beyond the bridge over the river itself.

Hike south on the paved trail, and in less than 1/4 mile you come to Roaring River Falls, a fairly short but exceptionally powerful waterfall in a dramatically rugged setting. The source of Roaring River is in the backcountry region of Cloud and Deadman canyons, a pair of exceptionally beautiful canyons.

Please note that it is not possible to hike up Roaring River from the falls. Several people have been injured and killed by trying to climb these steep cliffs.

Just north of the falls (back toward the parking area), you find the River Trail, marked by a sign which reads, "Zumwalt Meadow— Roads End."

At first the trail passes near the highway, which is a bit discouraging, but you soon enter a quieter area of the canyon; in fact, this trail is one of the most likely places in the canyon to spot a black bear. There are also several opportunities for fishing along the river here.

At 1 1/2 miles you reach the Zumwalt Bridge. Here you may cross over to the north side of the river and continue 1/4 mile to the Zumwalt Meadow parking area. The trail to Roads End, however, continues up canyon.

At about 1 3/4 miles, you reach Zumwalt Meadow. Green and lush, and surrounded by tall pines, this is one of the prettiest scenes in Kings Canyon. In the early days of Cedar Grove, it was one of the few places in the canyon for grazing.

It has been often said by cattlemen, in defense of their grazing practices, that cows don't conflict with deer because cows are grazers (meaning they eat grass), while deer are browsers (meaning they eat mostly shrubs). Here at Zumwalt Meadow you will most likely see deer, and they will most likely be grazing in the meadow. If you were to follow a cow around for a day, you would find that cattle also browse, on young oak seedlings, manzanita—anything palatable. So cattle and deer are both grazers and browsers, and deer do suffer in areas that are heavily grazed by cattle. That is one reason why the National Park Service has a policy of not permitting cattle grazing on meadows such as this one.

The trail now scrambles over talus slopes of large boulders that have tumbled down from the canyon walls above. At about 2 1/4 miles you come to a fork in the trail; the fork to the north follows the Zumwalt Meadow Loop, and leads you to the Zumwalt Meadow parking area; the trail up canyon leads you to Roads End.

You now follow closely along the banks of the river, where there are good pools for fishing, and swimming (but only when the water level is low).

At 2 1/2 miles you reach a footbridge. Cross over to the north side, and follow the trail less than 1/2 mile to the Roads End parking area.

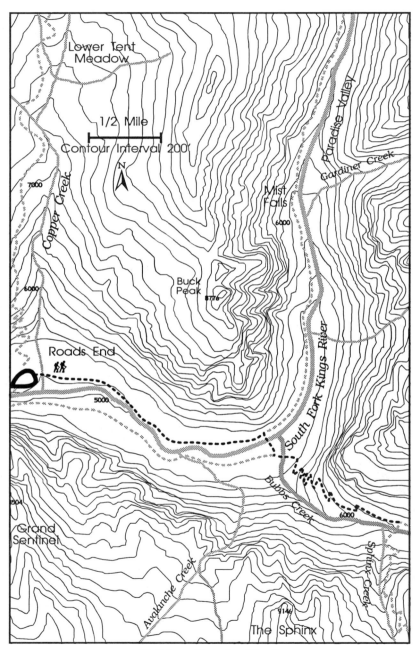

Bubbs Creek Trail

BUBBS CREEK TRAIL

DISTANCE: 4 Miles to Sphinx Creek
HIKING TIME: 2 1/2 Hours
STARTING ELEVATION: 5035´
HIGHEST ELEVATION: 6250´
DIFFICULTY: Moderate to Strenuous
USGS MAP: Marion Peak

There aren't many day hikes that can give you the feeling of being deep in the backcountry, but this trail is one of them. It's not as heavily-used as the Paradise Valley Trail, though it's distance and difficulty are similar.

Look for the trailhead at the east end of the parking area at Roads End, 5.6 miles from the Cedar Grove Ranger Station. At the trailhead there's an information booth manned by a park service employee.

The trail begins by crossing several small forks of Copper Creek. This area along Copper Creek was once a large Indian village site; a sharp eye can still find flakes of black obsidian used by the Indians for making arrowheads, knives, and scrapers.

The site of the old Kanawyers Store is just east of Copper Creek, and north of the trail. Peter Apoleon Kanawyer, known as "Pole" to his friends, was a prospector who filed a mining claim for copper ore near here in the 1880s. The site became a popular stopping point and supply station for cattleman, sheepherders and prospectors traveling in and out of the mountains, so Kanawyer, with the help of his wife, Viola, converted the mining claim into a store. John Muir once said he would walk the length of the Sierra for one of Mrs. Kanawyers pies. The store buildings were torn down about 1927, but at the Cedar

Grove Ranger Station you can see an interesting photograph of the Kanawyers Store when it was in its prime.

For the next mile or so the trail passes through a broad, flat, sandy area, with only a few scattered cedars and ponderosa pines. Here and there are house-size boulders that have tumbled down from the steep cliffs. Looking to the south you have a fine view of Grand Sentinel, which rises 3500 feet above the valley floor.

After the first mile, you enter a swampy area as the trail passes closer to the river. This is a good place to watch for wildlife, particularly deer and bear.

At 2 miles, elevation 5098 feet, you come to a trail junction. The trail to Paradise Valley turns to the north; the Bubbs Creek Trail continues east, and in just 200 feet you come to the Bailey Bridge. Cross the bridge over the South Fork of the Kings, and continue hiking through the cedar thicket; in less than 1/4 mile you come to a trail sign which reads, "Roads End 2.6 miles." But continue hiking east, crossing the four wooden bridges over Bubbs Creek.

The trail now begins climbing along the north side of Bubbs Creek, following short, fairly steep switchbacks, and allowing alternating views of the canyon toward Paradise Valley, and of the canyon toward Cedar Grove.

Bubbs Creek usually carries almost as much water as the South Fork of the Kings. It was named after John Bubbs, a cattleman and prospector who crossed over Kearsage Pass from the Owens Valley in 1864.

The trail passes near several pinyon pines, with short, bluish-green needles. Pinyons are fairly rare on the west side of the Sierra, but are more common on the east side and over much of the Great Basin. The pine nuts from pinyons are quite nutritious, and were an important source of food for the Indians, even though the pinyon trees only produce a crop in alternating years.

By 3 miles, elevation 5600 feet, you begin to have some views down into the Bubbs Creek gorge—large emerald-green pools, and white frothy waterfalls. The sides of the gorge have been fractured by the movement of glaciers down the canyon.

At this point you are almost directly beneath the Sphinx, the curious, double-topped granite formation named by John Muir after the famous Sphinx of Egypt.

By about 3 1/4 miles you reach the last of the switchbacks, and enter an area shaded by oaks and cedars. The trail soon draws close to the edge of Bubbs Creek, passing several pretty pools.

At about 3 3/4 miles, you are directly across from Sphinx Creek. Looking to the south, you may be able to see the Sphinx Creek Trail climbing precariously up the steep canyon wall. That airy trail leads over Avalanche Pass to Roaring River.

Now the trail levels off a bit, and at 4 miles, elevation 6250 feet, you reach the Sphinx Creek junction. This is a very pretty area where you might spend an entire day fishing or swimming. There are good campsites above the junction, as well as a log bridge giving access to the south side of the creek.

On your return route you can make a partial loop of this hike by taking the Sentinel Trail, which is described in that chapter.

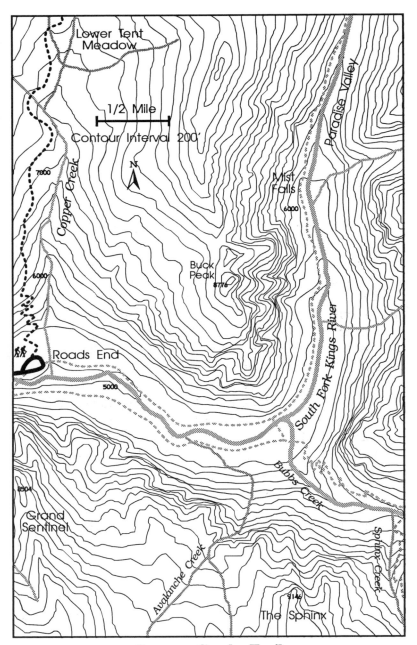

Copper Creek Trail

COPPER CREEK TRAIL

DISTANCE: 4 Miles to Lower Tent Meadow
HIKING TIME: 3 Hours
STARTING ELEVATION: 5035′
HIGHEST ELEVATION: 7825′
DIFFICULTY: Strenuous
USGS MAP: Marion Peak

Though at first glance the 2800-foot elevation gain on this trail is enough to give even an armchair hiker angina, the grade of the trail is not bad, and all things considered this hike is not as strenuous as some with less elevation gain.

Less ambitious hikers will enjoy hiking just a short distance up this trail, where excellent views of the valley can be had.

This trail can be hot and dry in the summer. Try to get an early start, and be sure to carry plenty of water—there are no creeks for the first 2 miles.

Look for the trailhead at the north side of the Roads End parking area, 5.6 miles from the Cedar Grove Ranger Station. The trailhead itself is marked by a large brown sign which reads, "Copper Creek Trail."

The trail begins climbing immediately up short switchbacks on the south-facing slope, passing through ponderosa pines, cedars and black oaks. You can see, and most likely hear, Copper Creek, which is just a few hundred feet to the east. At one time there was a large Indian village at Copper Creek, and even now you can sometimes find flakes of obsidian and soapstone beads there.

This is the kind of trail that makes you appreciate the work of trail construction crews. The terrain is so steep that extensive rock walls had to be built, all by hand, to create a path wide enough to walk on. A lot of sweat, blood and backaches went into this trail.

After just a few minutes of hiking, you already have an eagle's view both up and down Kings Canyon, and of the Grand Sentinel to the south. More to the southeast you can see the double-topped Sphinx, named by John Muir after the famous Sphinx of Egypt.

This is a fun trail to hike on a moonlit night. If you've never tried hiking in white-granite country by moonlight, it requires proper timing, both by the calendar, and by the watch, but it's an experience you will remember for a long time.

Looking down on Kings Canyon, you see a few sorrel-colored conifers here and there. These are dying trees that have been attacked by western bark beetles, a native insect that bores through the tree's bark to eat on the tender cambium layer. Normally, the tree's pitch oozes into the bore holes and kills the beetles before they do any damage, but during times of drought, or when the tree has been weakened in some other way, the tree isn't able to draw enough pitch to successfully evict the pests. Even so, it's not the beetles which kill the tree, but a fungus they carry with them. Once the tree has been infected with the fungus, it can't recover, and the tree inevitably dies. As late as the 1970s, the Park Service made a costly effort to eradicate bark beetles by cutting down infected trees and spraying them with pesticide; that effort had little effect, and today the Park's policy is that bark beetles are a naturally-occurring agent for removing weak or injured trees. Therefore, infected trees are no longer treated or removed.

In other words, it's perfectly normal to see dying trees in a healthy forest.

By 1/2 mile you are able to look down into the canyon of Copper Creek, though not all the way to the bottom.

At about 2 miles, elevation 6650 feet, you come to a small creek which usually flows year-round. This creek, marked by willows, currants and wild roses, drains the east side of North

Dome. Late in the summer the wild roses display large red rose hips, which, when dried, make an excellent tea.

The trail now has fewer switchbacks, and better shade.

At 3 1/2 miles, elevation 7520 feet, you come to a fork of Copper Creek. Here the trail dips 30 feet or so into the creek bottom, which is thick with willows. This is a cool spot to rest or have lunch under the aspens. Before you cross the creek, though, stop to look at the large granite rock south of the creek and just east of the trail. Here you can see several mortar holes used by the Indians for grinding seeds and acorns. Obviously, this trail was an ancient route into the high country.

At about 3 3/4 miles you come to a finger of Lower Tent Meadow, where there is a small campsite.

The trail now climbs sharply until you reach Lower Tent Meadow, 4 miles, elevation 7825 feet, where there are several good campsites near a fork of Copper Creek. The meadow itself is actually a network of several small stringer meadows.

Upper Tent Meadow, still a ways up the trail, received its name because of a large granite rock which, as one descends from Granite Pass, appears to be a white tent pitched in the meadow.

The truly hearty day hiker can continue on to Granite Basin, 10 miles, elevation 10,000 feet.

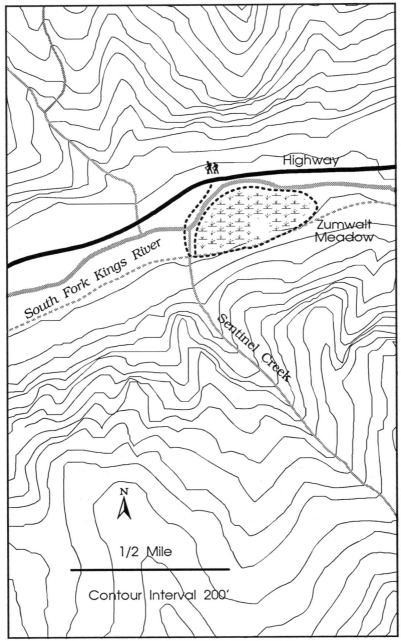

Zumwalt Meadow Loop

ZUMWALT MEADOW LOOP

DISTANCE: 1 1/2 Miles
HIKING TIME: 1 Hour
STARTING ELEVATION: 4950´
HIGHEST ELEVATION: 5000´
DIFFICULTY: Easy
USGS MAP: Marion Peak

Trails in Cedar Grove don't get any easier than the Zumwalt Meadow Loop. The route is practically flat, which is something of a rarity anywhere in the Sierra, and the loop is short enough that even young children can complete it. But the meadow and its surroundings are also exceptionally beautiful. First-time visitors to Cedar Grove should make this their first hike.

The Zumwalt Meadow parking area is 4.7 miles east of the Cedar Grove ranger station. The parking area is marked by a large brown sign.

This is a self-guided nature trail. For twenty-five cents you can buy a small pamphlet which guides you around the loop.

The flat between the parking area and the river was an Indian campsite at one time, as you can see by the mortar holes in the rocks. Black oaks are abundant here, and acorns from black oaks were the Indians favorite staple—sweeter than other acorns, they said. Also, there were pine nuts, currants, and manzanita berries, as well as fish from the river. The nearby meadow provided a reliable source of deer and other game, as well.

At 1/4 mile you cross on a suspension bridge to the south side of the river. The view up canyon here is one of the finest in all of Cedar Grove.

You now turn east and, looking to the north, you have a view of North Dome, elevation 8717 feet.

You cross Sentinel Creek, which is usually dry by late summer, and soon have a good view of Zumwalt Meadow. This is the only meadow of any size in Cedar Grove, and therefore it was very valuable to early cattle and sheep men. It takes its name from its one-time owner, Daniel P. Zumwalt, a Tulare County lawyer and land agent for the Southern Pacific Railroad.

Though the story is not entirely clear, it appears that Zumwalt played an important part in the establishment of Sequoia and General Grant National Parks; his motivation, apparently, was not so much an interest in conservation, but rather to protect the interests of the all-powerful Southern Pacific Railroad, which stood to gain financially if the vast timber resources in Sequoia and Kings Canyon were not harvested. At that time, the Southern Pacific was reaping huge profits in the development of central and southern California by charging high shipping costs on the lumber sent by their railroad from northern California.

After Zumwalt's death, the meadow fell into the hands of Jesse Agnew, who later became infamous for having killed the last grizzly bear in California, at Horse Corral Meadow in 1922. Agnew's daughter deeded the land to the Sierra Club, which eventually donated it to the Park Service.

Continuing up canyon, you pass near large granite boulders that have tumbled down from the cliffs above, as well as a talus slope of fractured rocks. Here you see young maple trees, not a very common tree in the Sierra, sprouting almost everywhere.

You now approach the edge of Zumwalt Meadow. This is a good place to spot deer and other wildlife, as well as a good place to rest or have lunch.

At about 3/4 miles you come to a trail junction, and turn north, following the edge of the meadow toward the river. This stretch of river is fairly tranquil—something not easy to find on the turbulent Kings.

The trail now crosses the meadow on a wooden causeway, built there to protect the fragile meadow vegetation.

At the junction you turn right, and complete the 1/2 mile back to the parking area.

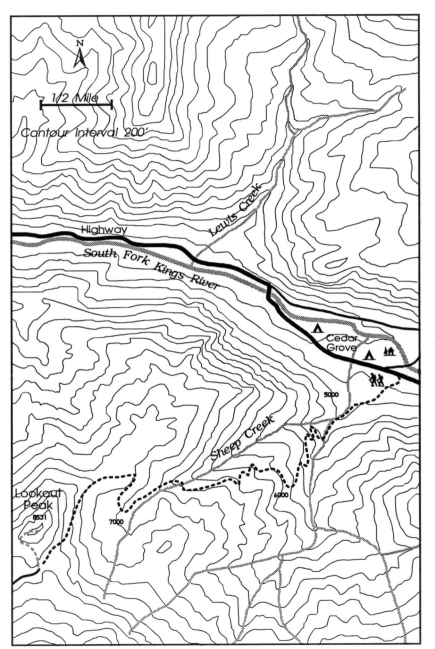

Don Cecil Trail

DON CECIL TRAIL

From Cedar Grove

DISTANCE: 1 Mile to Sheep Creek; 5 3/4 Miles
    to Summit Meadow

HIKING TIME: 1/2 Hour to Sheep Creek; 4
    Hours to Summit Meadow

STARTING ELEVATION: 4650´

HIGHEST ELEVATION: 5200´ at Sheep Creek;
    8000´ at Summit Meadow

DIFFICULTY: Easy to Sheep Creek; Strenuous
    to Summit Meadow

USGS MAP: Marion Peak

To hike the Don Cecil Trail is to go back in time and see
Cedar Grove the way the first settlers saw it.

Imagine Cedar Grove without the modern highway and
the bridges across the Kings River. How would you get here?
The route the highway follows today would be nothing but a
vertical cliff above a raging river. And to try to ford the Kings
in spring, or even midsummer in some years, would be un-
thinkably dangerous.

The answer is that you would get to Cedar Grove by way
of Sheep Creek, a natural, fairly gentle route that has been used
by the deer and bear for thousands of years.

The trailhead for the Don Cecil Trail is 1/4 mile east of the
turnoff to the Cedar Grove ranger station. Look for the trailhead sign on the south side of the highway. There are small
turnouts, both east and west of the trailhead. Or, you can begin
at the amphitheater next to the ranger station.

The trail begins climbing moderately from the valley floor, passing through black oaks, cedars and ponderosa pines. Because of the north-facing slope, this trail isn't quite as hot and dry as some trails in Cedar Grove, but it's still best to get any early morning start, or an early evening start. And be sure to carry water.

At 1/4 mile you cross the access road to the water storage tank for Cedar Grove. Pick up the trail again on the other side.

By 3/4 miles you have entered the Sheep Creek drainage, and you begin to hear the sound of the creek, which flows year-round. Looking back to the north, you have a view of the white granite peaks of the Monarch Divide.

The trail now descends, and at 1 mile, elevation 5200 feet, you reach the Sheep Creek bridge. This is a very pretty spot, with a small waterfall above the wooden foot bridge, and a few alders growing from the rocky creek bed. Sheep Creek is the water source for Cedar Grove—no swimming, please.

The name Sheep Creek is perhaps an unfortunate one; out of the thousands of years this drainage was used as an animal migration route, it was used for herding sheep for just a few decades. The trail itself is named for Don Cecil, an early sheepherder.

Unless you're looking for a vigorous workout, it doesn't make a lot of sense to hike all the way to Lookout Peak, since nowadays you can drive to within a few hundred yards of it by way of Forest Service roads out of the Big Meadow area. An interesting and fairly easy hike, however, is to have somebody drop you off at Summit Meadow (near Lookout Peak), and hike down the Don Cecil Trail to Cedar Grove. That hike is described in detail in the Monarch Wilderness section of this guidebook, under the chapter on the Don Cecil Trail.

Still, many hikers will want to explore this trail above the Sheep Creek bridge, and the following description is for them:

The trail follows fairly steep switchbacks, giving ever more impressive views of the Monarch Divide to the north.

At about 2 miles, elevation 6000 feet, looking to the northeast, you have a view of Mt. Clarence King, 12,905 feet, one of the most handsome and distinctively-shaped peaks in the southern Sierra. It's named after the first director of the U.S. Geological Survey.

You now cross the ridge separating the two main forks of Sheep Creek. The going here is slow and steep.

As an indication of how old this trail is, on some of the mature trees you can see rectangular blaze marks that have almost completely grown over with bark.

The trail climbs a bit less steeply now, and at about 3 1/2 miles you can begin to hear the west fork of Sheep Creek, still several hundred feet below. Looking to the southwest, you can now see glimpses of Lookout Peak through the trees.

At 4 miles, elevation 6990 feet, you cross the west fork of Sheep Creek, where there are currants, red willows, and ferns growing along the banks. This makes a fine place to rest.

The trail now leaves Sheep Creek, and begins climbing the ridge below Lookout Peak.

At about 4 3/4 miles, elevation 7200 feet, you begin the long but final traverse. Here you have excellent views of the Sierra crest to the east, of Cedar Grove below, and of the Monarch Divide to the north.

And at 5 3/4 miles, elevation 8000 feet, you reach the saddle and small parking area at Summit Meadow. You can continue on the Lookout Peak Trail, which is described in that chapter, you can return to Cedar Grove by the way you came, or, with a bit of previous planning, you can meet your ride here at Summit Meadow. For directions on how to reach the Summit Meadow trailhead by car, see the chapter on the Lookout Peak Trail.

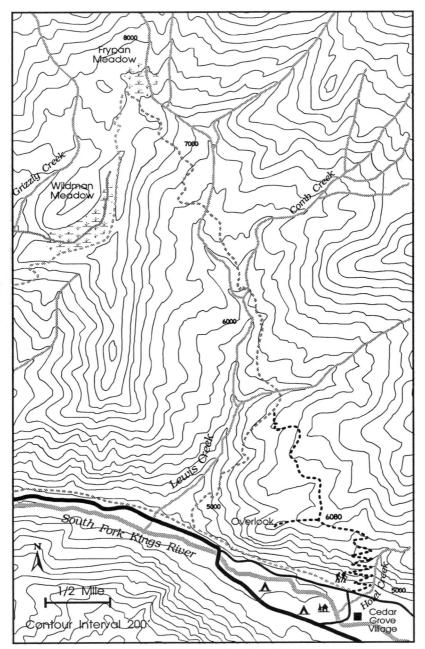

Hotel Creek Trail

HOTEL CREEK TRAIL

DISTANCE: 2 1/2 Miles to the Overlook
HIKING TIME: 2 Hours
STARTING ELEVATION: 4660´
HIGHEST ELEVATION: 6000´ at the Overlook
DIFFICULTY: Strenuous
USGS MAP: Marion Peak

The Hotel Creek Trail's major attraction is an overlook which gives an excellent view of almost the entire Cedar Grove area. Most of the work involved is in climbing to the rim of the canyon, where the overlook is located. But once you have reached that point, you can easily hike over to the Lewis Creek Trail and make a loop hike back to Cedar Grove, if you wish.

This is one of the hottest trails out of Cedar Grove, so try to get an early start, and carry plenty of water—there is no reliable source for water along the way.

The Hotel Creek Trail begins 0.3 miles west of the Cedar Grove pack station. (From the ranger station, or the market, simply follow the road signs to the pack station.) There's a small parking area at the trailhead, which is marked with a large brown sign.

As the trail leaves the parking area, notice the metal sign which reads, "Stock Route to Lewis Creek Trail." If you make the complete loop by way of Lewis Creek, that is the trail that will return you to this point.

The trail climbs a series of short, fairly steep switchbacks, passing through canyon live oak, manzanita, black oak, and ponderosa pines.

After less than 1/4 mile, the trail passes within a few hundred feet of Hotel Creek. (At this point the stock route continues across the creek to the pack station.) Since this is the closest you will get to Hotel Creek on this hike, you might want to walk over and see the creek now.

Hotel Creek was named for a "hotel," or camp, at Cedar Grove in the 1890s, run by John Fox and Hugh Robinson.

It's interesting to note that the Indians located one of their major village sites in Cedar Grove at the base of Hotel Creek, indicating that the trail you are now hiking was probably used by the Indians as a major route into the high country. You can still find the village site, which is just east of the pack station, by looking for the rock with mortar holes, which the Indians used for grinding acorns.

As you continue up the trail, looking across the canyon to the south, you can see the Sheep Creek drainage. Looking to the east, on the south side of Kings Canyon, you can see the Roaring River drainage. The peak to the east of it is Palmer Mountain.

The trail continues climbing short, steep switchbacks, with very little variation.

At 1 3/4 miles, the trail finally begins leveling off as you reach a bench on the rim of the canyon. The trail makes one long and final switchback, passing through an area that was burned by the Lewis Creek Fire of 1980.

At 2 miles, elevation 6080 feet, you come to a junction marked by a metal sign. The mileages given on the sign are a bit confusing: The Overlook is 1/2 mile, not 1 mile; and it is 4 miles to Lewis Creek, but only 1 1/2 miles to the Lewis Creek Trail from this junction.

Continuing on to the Overlook, the trail descends slightly, following a short ridge which extends away from the bench.

From the Overlook you can look down canyon for several miles, and looking up canyon you can see as far as the junction of Bubbs Creek with the South Fork of the Kings. In the distant east you can see some of the high peaks on the Great Western Divide; the long flat mountain is known as Table Mountain,

13,630 feet. Looking to the north, you can see some of the white peaks along the Monarch Divide.

You can now return to Cedar Grove by the same route, or you can continue on to the Lewis Creek Trail and make a loop hike back to Cedar grove.

Continuing on to Lewis Creek, from the junction at 6080 feet, you turn to the north, passing through scattered ponderosa pines, and a dense carpet of kit-kit-dizze. As you can see, this area was burned in the Lewis Creek Fire of 1980.

The trail dips and rises some, and by 2 1/2 miles you are able to see into the lower Lewis Creek drainage.

The trail begins to descend into a small fork of Lewis Creek, but before reaching the creek you meet the Lewis Creek Trail, on a flat covered with ponderosa pines and cedars. The junction, at 3 1/2 miles, elevation 5600 feet, is marked by a metal sign. Here you can turn to the southwest and follow the Lewis Creek Trail back to Cedar Grove, or, you can continue up the Lewis Creek Trail, which is described in that chapter.

If you return to Cedar Grove by way of the Lewis Creek Trail, follow the steep trail 2 miles to the Lewis Creek Trailhead, elevation 4550 feet. From the Lewis Creek Trailhead you can follow either the road or the stock route 1 1/2 miles back to the Hotel Creek Trailhead. Distance for the entire Hotel Creek-Lewis Creek Loop is 7 miles.

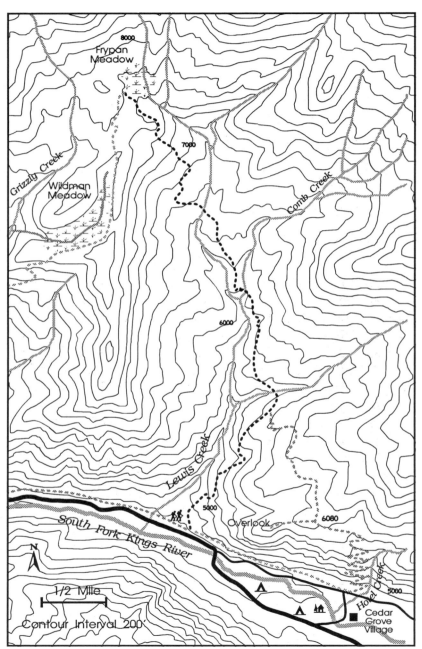

Lewis Creek Trail

LEWIS CREEK TRAIL

DISTANCE: 4 3/4 Miles to Lewis Creek; 6 Miles to Frypan Meadow

HIKING TIME: 4 Hours to Lewis Creek; 5 Hours to Frypan Meadow

STARTING ELEVATION: 4550´

HIGHEST ELEVATION: 6500´ at Lewis Creek; 7760´ at Frypan Meadow

DIFFICULTY: Strenuous

USGS MAP: Marion Peak

The first couple miles of the Lewis Creek Trail are among the least exciting in Cedar Grove. But those day hikers who persist as far as Comb Creek, or even the Lewis Creek crossing, will be delighted by these cool, clear creeks in fairly remote settings. Only fit and determined hikers will reach Frypan Meadow, but from there you have the option of returning by way of Wildman Meadow and the Deer Cove Trail, thus making a long loop hike.

In the summer this trail is hot and dry much of the way, so try to get an early start, and be sure to carry water.

The trailhead, marked by a large brown sign, is on the highway 1.3 miles west of the Cedar Grove Village turnoff. The trail begins on the north side of the highway, but the large parking area is on the south side of the highway.

The trail begins by climbing steeply through cedars, manzanita, and kit-kit-dizze, following a route 400 feet above Lewis Creek.

During much of this hike you will be passing through areas that were burned in the Lewis Creek Fire of September 1980. That fire was started accidentally by a park service trail crew blasting rocks along this trail. Most of the Lewis Creek drainage at that time was a thick snarl of dead or very old manzanita and buck brush. A fire here was inevitable, though the Park Service would have preferred to burn it under cooler, prescribed conditions. Some of the hotter areas of the fire were badly charred, and hundreds of trees were killed. In other areas of the fire, though, you can see that only the old brush was removed and that many young pine seedlings are now growing vigorously. The manzanita, black oaks, and buck brush have been re-invigorated by the fire.

Ironically, the cost of extinguishing the Lewis Creek Fire was $1.1 million, enough to fund a prescribed-burn program in this park for several years.

By 1 mile, elevation 5200 feet, you begin having views of the Monarch Divide, to the north.

At 2 miles, elevation 5800 feet, on a flat covered with ponderosa pines and cedars, you come to a junction marked by a metal sign. Here you have the option of returning to Cedar Grove (3 1/2 miles from this junction) by way of the Hotel Creek Trail, which is described in that chapter.

Continuing on the Lewis Creek Trail, you now descend to a small creek in a deeply-eroded ravine. Here you are likely to find water, even late in the year.

After climbing out of the ravine, the trail contours gently around the mountainside, until at 3 1/2 miles, elevation 6080 feet, you reach Comb Creek, which carries almost as much water as Lewis Creek. This pretty site is heavily wooded with ponderosa pines and cedars, and makes a good destination for a day hike. There are campsites here where you can rest or have lunch, and there are several nice pools along the creek.

The trail now climbs steeply, as you cross the ridge separating Comb Creek from Lewis Creek. This is one of the most badly-scorched areas of the Lewis Creek Fire, with a great number of dead trees.

At 4 3/4 miles, elevation 6500 feet, you arrive at Lewis Creek, named for Frank and Jeff Lewis, who were early sheepmen and prospectors in this area.

This site is even prettier than Comb Creek. The water has eroded the granite creek bed into sensuous pools that make perfect bathtubs in late summer. You have your choice of sun or shade for a noontime nap.

Lewis Creek is the most sensible destination for a day hike on this trail. But for those hikers who have no sense, the trail continues.

The next couple of miles are the steepest climbing on this trail. At 5 miles, looking back to the southeast as you pause to catch your breath, you can see the Great Western Divide. Looking to the north, you are now almost directly beneath the Monarch Divide, with white granite faces separated by broad patches of green timber. Notice the avalanche chutes on the face of the divide; some of the chutes have graceful glacial moraines along one side of them.

Gradually, the trail begins turning to the northwest. (Note that the cutoff to Wildman Meadow, shown on the USGS map at 7200 feet, is no longer maintained and is difficult to find.)

At 7600 feet the trail begins to level off, as you enter a dense forest of red firs. The ground vegetation changes to red willow, thimbleberry, and lupine.

And at 6 miles, elevation 7760 feet, you come to a junction on a dusty knoll and marked by a metal sign. Frypan Meadow is just a few hundred feet to the north. It's a lush green meadow, of moderate size, apparently named for its shape.

You can now return to Cedar Grove by the same route, or you can cross the ridge to Wildman Meadow and descend to Cedar Grove by way of the Deer Cove Trail.

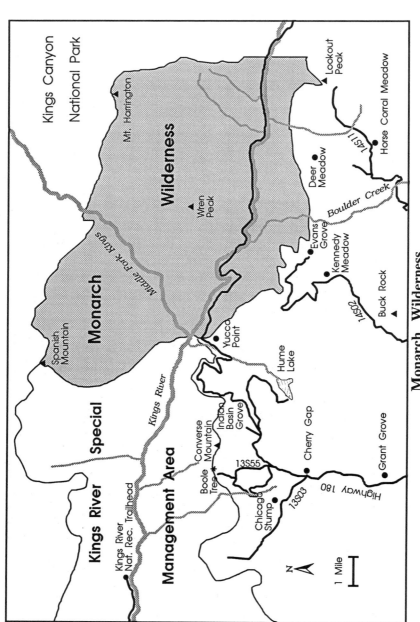

Monarch Wilderness

INTRODUCTION
TO
THE MONARCH WILDERNESS

Just by looking at it on a map, and judging by its size, one might think that environmentalists won a major victory when the 45,000-acre Monarch Wilderness was established in 1984 as part of the California Wilderness Act. In fact, most of the Monarch Wilderness is so steep that neither man nor beast can walk on it without being roped in. The boundaries were carefully drawn to exclude valuable timber and grazing resources, and the lower Kings River canyon, which was coveted as a dam site, was left out as well.

Most regrettable among those areas left out of the wilderness are: Converse Mountain, Evans Grove, Deer Meadow, Deer Meadow Grove, upper Lightning Creek, and half of Lookout Peak. Several of the trails in this guidebook pass through or near these areas, so hikers can decide for themselves whether or not Congress erred in excluding them from the wilderness.

Also included in this section of the guidebook is a 60,000-acre Special Management Area adjacent to the Monarch Wilderness. This Special Management Area is to be managed with an emphasis on recreation, and no new timber sales are supposed to take place within its boundaries. This area, which is extremely valuable as winter habitat for the Kings River deer herd, can be seen from the Cabin Creek Grove Trail, and especially from the Kings River National Recreation Trail, which passes through its heart.

This section of the guidebook also includes an area that was a hundred years too late for wilderness designation, Converse Basin, which at one time contained the largest stand of giant sequoias in the world. That area was heavily logged around the turn of this century, and now only one first-generation giant sequoia is left, the Boole Tree.

Today the Converse Basin area makes an interesting, if disturbing, contrast with the nearby Grant Grove area. In Grant Grove we have some of the world's largest and finest stands of giant sequoias, trees so beautiful and rare that millions of people travel here every year to see them. In Converse Basin, nearly one hundred years after the forest was ravaged, all we have to show for it is a 5,000-acre scar which still hasn't healed.

Although many hikers will find fault with the logging practices all over Sequoia National Forest, it's only fair to point out that the Forest Service was not responsible for what happened at Converse Basin. The logging at Converse Basin took place in the years between 1897 and 1907, when the land was still in private hands. The U.S. Forest Service wasn't even established until 1905.

It's also important to understand, though, that Converse Basin had originally been public lands. All over the West, American citizens could legally apply for timber claims of no more than 160 acres. In an era of poor government regulation, timber barons who understood the weaknesses of the law paid dishonest citizens to file fraudulent claims, which were later turned over to the barons themselves. In this way the land's resources were stolen from the American people, and were destroyed.

Those hikers who care about the public lands as more than just recreational opportunities for a day's outing should visit the Converse Basin, particularly the Chicago Stump Trail and the Boole Tree Trail, and learn from the mistakes that were made there.

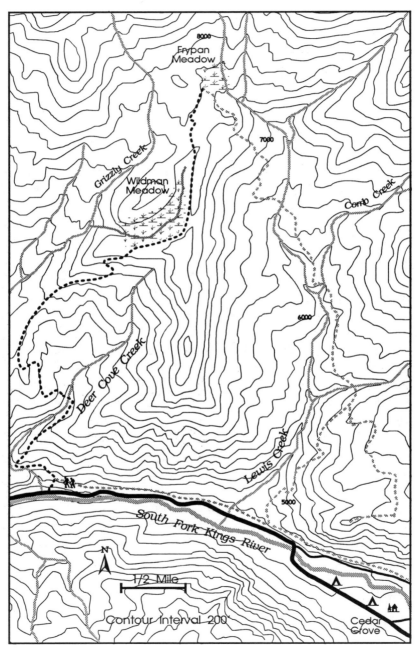

Deer Cove Trail

DEER COVE TRAIL

DISTANCE: 2 Miles to Deer Cove; 7 miles to
Wildman Meadow

HIKING TIME: 1 1/2 Hours to Deer Cove; 5
Hours to Wildman Meadow

STARTING ELEVATION: 4400′

HIGHEST ELEVATION: 5600′ at Deer Cove;
7600′ above Wildman Meadow

DIFFICULTY: Strenuous

USGS MAP: Marion Peak

Although this trail is in the Monarch Wilderness, the trailhead is just outside the boundary of Kings Canyon National Park, and most hikers using this trail will probably be staying at Cedar Grove.

For those energetic hikers looking for a challenge, note that it's possible to make a 15 1/2-mile loop by way of this trail and the Lewis Creek Trail.

Because of the south-facing slope, this trail is hot and dry. Be sure to carry water, and try to get an early-morning start.

The Deer Cove trailhead can be found on Highway 180, 2.7 miles west of the Cedar Grove Village turnoff. Look for the parking area on the north side of the road, where there is also a trail register.

Just a few feet up the trail, you cross the stock route which leads back to the Cedar Grove pack station.

The trail follows short, steep switchbacks through manzanita, cedars, and black oaks. The ground cover is mostly bear clover, sometimes known as mountain misery, or by its Miwok Indian name, kit-kit-dizze.

At about 1/2 mile, the trail passes above a large spring which gushes from the mountainside and immediately become a full-size creek.

After gaining a few hundred feet in elevation, looking back to the southwest you can see the Lightning Creek drainage, which is also in the Monarch Wilderness and is accessible from the Big Meadow Road. Looking due south you can see Lookout Peak, elevation 8581 feet, which is also accessible from the Big Meadow Road.

At about 1 1/2 miles, elevation 5600 feet, the trail levels off somewhat as you enter the Deer Cove Creek drainage. Here there are large conifers shading the trail.

Looking to the northeast you soon have an impressive view of Kennedy Mountain, elevation 11433 feet. This strikingly handsome white-granite peak is on the backbone of the Monarch Divide.

And at about 2 miles, elevation 5600 feet, you arrive at Deer Cove Creek in a steep and narrow drainage that is heavily wooded with Jeffrey pines, cedars and firs.

Most day hikers will be satisfied with having reached Deer Cove. But for those continuing on to Wildman Meadow, the trail now makes a long, steep, winding ascent of the southwest-facing slope, passing through ponderosa and Jeffrey pines, blacks oaks, chinquapin, and manzanita. There is no water available before Wildman Meadow.

At about 5 1/2 miles, elevation 6400 feet, you reach a sandy knoll from which you have a good view into the rugged Grizzly Creek drainage, to the west. (Note that the trail shown on the USGS map descending to Grizzly Creek is no longer maintained.) The curious black and red granite formation on the ridge to the west is known as the Grand Dike. "Dike" is a geological term for igneous rock that has solidified in a vertical fissure.

The trail now continues its steep ascent, until you reach the top of the ridge at about 6 1/2 miles, elevation 7600 feet. As you cross over to the north-facing slope, notice how the chaparral-type vegetation ends abruptly, and you enter a forest of large firs.

A quick and easy descent brings you to Wildman Meadow, 7 miles, elevation 7500 feet. Here you find a large stock camp on the edge of the meadow, which is marked by a wooden sign nailed to a fir tree. (Note that the location of Wildman Meadow is marked incorrectly on the USGS map.)

Wildman Meadow was named by John and Frank Lewis: "About 1881 brother Jeff and I camped there with a band of sheep," Frank Lewis said. "After dark we were startled by a lot of unearthly yells, like someone in distress. After spending a large part of that night, we were unable to locate anyone and finally concluded it must have been a wildman, and so named the meadow. Later we found the noise was caused by a peculiar-looking owl."

If you choose to continue on to Frypan Meadow, the trail skirts the edge of Wildman Meadow before turning north. Just a few hundred feet after crossing the head of the meadow, you come to a trail junction, marked by an old wooden sign nailed to a tree. Burns Meadow and Happy Gap are to the northwest; Frypan Meadow is to the northeast.

After climbing a short ridge, elevation 7840 feet, you leave the Monarch Wilderness and enter Kings Canyon National Park.

Descending from the ridge, at 8 1/4 miles, elevation 7760 feet, you come to a junction on a dusty knoll, marked by a metal sign. Frypan Meadow is just a few hundred feet to the north. It's a lush green meadow, of moderate size, apparently named for its shape.

The Lewis Creek Trail now returns you to the highway (6 miles from this point.) You then follow either the stock route or the highway 1 1/2 miles back to the Deer Cove trailhead, where you began. The complete mileage for the Deer Cove-Lewis Creek Loop is 15 1/2 miles.

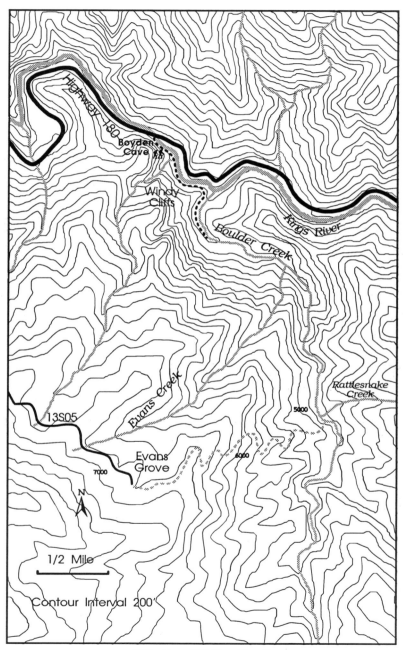

Windy Cliffs Trail

WINDY CLIFFS TRAIL

To Boulder Creek

DISTANCE: 1 1/2 Miles to Boulder Creek
HIKING TIME: 1 Hour
STARTING ELEVATION: 3062′
HIGHEST ELEVATION: 3450′
DIFFICULTY: Moderate
USGS MAP: Tehipite Dome

Before Highway 180 was completed to Cedar Grove, in 1939, this trail was one route into Cedar Grove. The trail is now in poor condition, and is no longer maintained, but experienced and cautious hikers can still follow its route as far as Boulder Creek. This trail is not suitable for children, or for novice hikers who do not feel comfortable in steep, rugged terrain.

The trail begins at the Boyden Cave parking area. (Boyden Cave is on Highway 180, 19.3 miles from the Grant Grove Visitor Center, or 9.5 miles from the Cedar Grove Village turnoff.) Look for the trailhead at the east end of the parking area, near the snack bar. Tours through Boyden cave leave from this point every hour, which is why the trail is chained off. The Windy Cliffs Trail is not part of the cave concession, so it is permissible to go around the chain; but before proceeding up the trail it would be courteous of you to stop at the snack bar and explain to the concessioner that you are hiking to Boulder Creek.

Follow the paved trail for less than 1/4 mile to the first switchback. Here the trail to Boyden Cave turns uphill, but the Windy Cliffs trail continues to the east. A sign posted at this point reads, "Hazardous Trail Not Maintained."

The first few hundred feet of trail beyond the sign are paved, with a guard rail. After that, however, the trail quickly narrows into a steep footpath. Notice the small sign, posted on a live oak, which marks the boundary of the Monarch Wilderness.

The trail passes through live oak, red bud, laurel, yucca, and some poison oak. Directly ahead you can see the 2,000-foot marble walls of the Windy Cliffs.

You soon cross Windy Gulch, which has a bed of blue marble boulders. Notice the redwood logs that have washed down from the Windy Gulch Grove of giant sequoias. You can explore a short way up Windy Gulch, but note that, unlike most granite, the marble formations are loose and fracture easily. There have been climbing fatalities in this area, caused by the loose marble. Do not climb here!

The marble formation at Windy Gulch is riddled with a network of caves, including Boyden Cave, which was discovered in 1907 by J.P. "Putt" Boyden. Boyden was a logger working at the lumber camps at Hume Lake. On his day off, he hiked to the bottom of Kings Canyon to go on a fishing expedition, and while hiking the rugged canyon floor discovered the entrance to the popular cave which now bears his name. (Boyden, by the way, later froze to death in a blizzard in 1916.)

Just above Boyden Cave is the entrance to Church Cave which, at 480 feet, is the deepest cave in California, as well as the second longest. (The longest is Lilburn Cave, in Redwood Canyon.)

The trail now follows the steep hillside above the Kings River and Highway 180. Looking to the east you can see part of the old trail, nearly hidden in the brush.

At about 1 mile you can look down into the canyon ahead of you and see Boulder Creek. Here the trail leaves the Kings River and turns south, into the Boulder Creek canyon.

As the trail climbs slightly, you can look up the canyon toward the gnarled and rugged marble cliffs.

You soon begin to see large pools in Boulder Creek, as well as short waterfalls. The trail now dips and rises, passing through some dense thickets of live oaks and nutmeg trees.

And at 1 1/2 miles, elevation 3450 feet, you arrive at Boulder Creek, where there are flat places along the creek where you can rest.

Here, in the very steep and rugged canyon, you see three old bridge abutments. The bridge washed out long ago, and the trail is no longer passable beyond this point. The canyon is very narrow, while the Boulder Creek watershed is really quite large; therefore, during times of heavy rainfall, the creek at this point is extremely swift and turbulent.

Use extreme caution here on the steep and slippery banks, particularly in the spring and early summer when the water level is high.

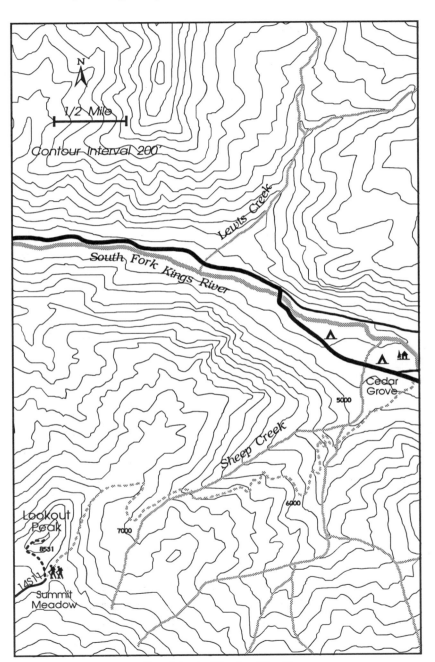

Lookout Peak Trail

LOOKOUT PEAK TRAIL

DISTANCE: 3/4 Miles

HIKING TIME: 30 Minutes

STARTING ELEVATION: 8000´

HIGHEST ELEVATION: 8531´

DIFFICULTY: Moderate

USGS MAP: Marion Peak

Even though Lookout Peak isn't really high enough to truly be considered a peak, the view of Kings Canyon from its summit is outstanding. The trail is short but steep, and some hands-and-knees scrambling is necessary to reach the top.

On the Generals Highway, drive south 6.9 miles from the Grant Grove Visitor Center, or north 4.8 miles from Stony Creek, to Big Meadow turnoff (forest service road 14S11). Turn east, reset your odometer, and drive 10.4 miles to Horse Corral Meadow.

At Horse Corral Meadow you continue driving in a northeasterly direction, following the dirt road (14S11). The road is not marked beyond this point; at each junction try to follow the most heavily-used road. After driving a total of 12.5 miles, you begin to have a view of the Monarch Divide to the north, and of Lookout Peak to the northeast. It's the peak directly in front of you with the two large microwave reflector towers on its summit. (The towers provide Cedar Grove with telephone service.)

At 14.1 miles, the road crosses the upper end of Summit Meadow. On your left, to the north, is a large dirt parking area.

Looking to the northeast you can see several signs marking the Don Cecil Trail, which descends to Cedar Grove. The Lookout Point Trail, however, is to the northwest.

The poorly-maintained trail begins by heading almost straight uphill. Look for the old blaze marks on the trees.

The trail soon traverses around to the southwest face of the peak, passing through ponderosa pines, manzanita and buck brush.

Near the top, the trail passes near some very large and oddly-eroded granite boulders.

About 200 feet below the summit, the trail fades away to nothing, and you have to pick your way over and through the boulders to reach the top. Be careful.

As you can see, the unobstructed view from Lookout Peak is due to the fact that the summit juts out away from the ridge behind it. You can see almost all of Cedar Grove, the crest of the Sierra, as well as part of the Great Western Divide. Everything to the east is Kings Canyon National Park, while most of what you see to the north is part of the Monarch Wilderness.

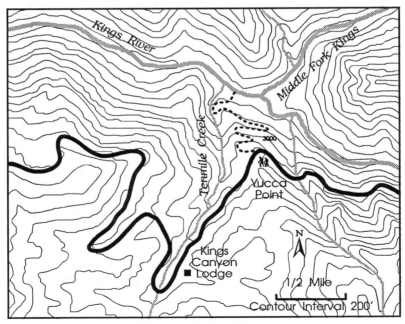

Yucca Point Trail

YUCCA POINT TRAIL

DISTANCE: 2 Miles

HIKING TIME: 1 Hour on the Return Trip

STARTING ELEVATION: 3400´

LOWEST ELEVATION: 2250´

DIFFICULTY: Strenuous on the Return Trip

USGS MAP: Tehipite Dome

This trail is very popular with fishermen, who value the excellent flyfishing along this remote stretch of the Kings River. But hikers of all sorts will be impressed by the dramatic views of the canyon, and by the power and beauty of the Kings.

Fishermen, take note: The Kings River, from Pine Flat Reservoir upstream to the western boundary of Kings Canyon National Park, is officially designated by the State of California as wild trout water. The river here is managed for its wild strain of streambed trout, without any domestic stocking.

During the winter months Highway 180 is closed below the Hume Lake turnoff. Call the Sequoia and Kings National Park headquarters, at 209-565-3341, to find out if the road is open.

Because of the low elevation, this trail can be quite hot in the summer. If you're hiking here in the summer, be sure to get an early start. Also, this is rattlesnake and tick country, so be on the lookout for those two hazards.

From the Grant Grove Visitor Center, drive north on Highway 180 13.5 miles. Or, from the turnoff to Cedar Grove Village, drive west 14.8 miles. The trailhead is marked by a wooden sign. There's a small parking area on the west side of the road, but if you're coming from Grant Grove, rather than cross the highway on a blind curve, it's better to drive another 0.1 miles to a large turnout, turn around, then return to the Yucca

Point trailhead. Be sure to leave room in the parking area for other vehicles.

The trail descends steeply, following short switchbacks through chaparral, consisting of laurel, redbud, live oak, manzanita, mountain mahogany, and of course, yucca. There's also some poison oak here and there, though it's easy to avoid. The trail is in good condition, but keeping the brush pruned back will always be a problem for trail maintenance crews here.

The drainage you see to the west is Tenmile Creek. When the Hume Lake area was logged in the first decade of this century, a wooden flume for carrying the milled lumber followed the general course of Tenmile Creek to the Kings River, and then on to the town of Sanger, in the San Joaquin Valley.

To the north, looming over the Kings River, is Spanish Mountain. If you consider Kings Canyon as being measured from the top of Spanish Mountain down to the river's bed, then this canyon is 7891 feet deep, making it one of the deepest canyons in North America.

By 1/4 mile, looking down into the canyon, you can see the confluence of the South Fork and the Middle Fork of the Kings River—a very impressive sight. In the spring and early summer, this is one of the most powerful rivers in the southern Sierra. By late summer, when the water level has receded, there are some very large, emerald-green pools that are a delight for fishermen and swimmers alike.

By 1/2 mile you have a good view up the South Fork of the Kings to Windy Cliffs, the large bluish marble formation where Boyden Cave is located.

You begin to see a few buckeye trees along the trail, now. In the spring these beautiful trees have brilliant-green leaves, and long white flower clusters. In the summer, when buckeyes go dormant, the leaves turn a rust color, and by fall only the large brown seed pods remain hanging from the branches. The buckeye seeds are poisonous in their natural form, but the

Indians used them for an emergency source of food by grinding the seeds and leaching out the strong tannic acid.

At about 1 1/2 miles, elevation 2550 feet, you have a good view of a 200-foot waterfall on Tenmile Creek. (At this point a non-maintained footpath leaves the main trail and descends steeply to Tenmile Creek. That footpath continues on the other side of the creek, but it is very brushy, and not recommended for hiking.)

Continuing down the main trail, you have a view far up the Middle Fork, to Tehipite Dome, a large, white-granite extrusion which guards over the Tehipite Valley like Half Dome in Yosemite. There is no trail leading from the confluence up canyon to Tehipite Valley, but some of the place names—Tombstone Ridge, and Gorge of Despair—give you a pretty good idea of what the terrain along the Middle Fork is like.

And at 2 miles, elevation 2250 feet, you reach the Kings River at the confluence of the Middle and South Forks, in the heart of some of the most godawful rugged country found anywhere in the West—hot, dry, rocky, rattlesnake infested, but with a magical green ribbon of life flowing through the middle of it.

As you can see by the high-water marks, there are times when this river carries a huge volume of water. There are non-maintained footpaths leading both up and down the canyon, but use extreme caution here, particularly when the water level is high. Late in the summer, there's a sandy beach here beside a large clear pool.

If you aren't lucky enough to catch any fish, don't go home empty handed. On your way back up the trail, gather a few laurel leaves, which are the same as the bay leaves used for cooking, though this variety is several times more potent than the variety sold in grocery stores.

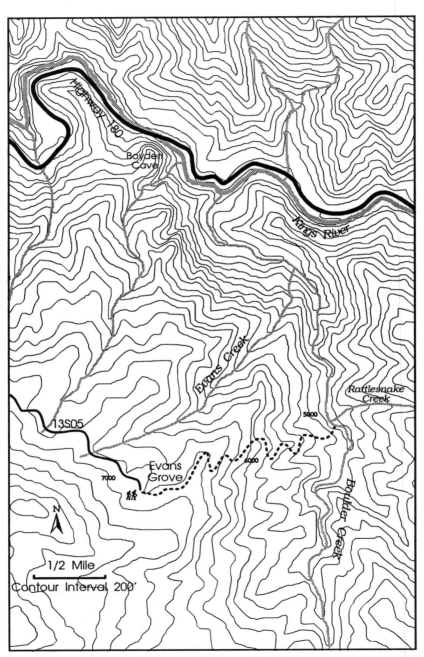

Evans Grove Trail

EVANS GROVE TRAIL

DISTANCE: 3/4 Miles to the edge of Evans
    Grove; 3 Miles to Boulder Creek

HIKING TIME: 1/2 Hour to the edge of Evans
    Grove; 1 1/2 Hours to Boulder Creek

STARTING ELEVATION: 7520′

LOWEST ELEVATION: 4800′ at Boulder Creek

DIFFICULTY: Easy to the edge of Evans Grove;
    Strenuous returning from Boulder Creek

USGS MAP: Tehipite Dome

You have to drive 15 miles on windy logging roads to find this trailhead, but the reward is a remote sequoia grove in an area not many people get a chance to see. The short hike through Evans Grove is peaceful and easy, but if you choose to descend into the steep Boulder Creek canyon, be prepared for a tough hike back out.

It is strongly recommended that you do not try to find this trailhead unless you have the current map for Sequoia National Forest, which can be purchased at any park service visitor center.

On the Generals Highway, 6.1 miles south of the Grant Grove Visitor Center, or 8.1 miles north of Stony Creek Village, take the Hume Lake—Quail Flat turnoff. At the turnoff, reset your odometer, and take the road to Weston Meadow and Burton Meadow (Road 14S02). The paved road is narrow and windy; keep your speed down, and stay on your own side of the road.

At 5.6 miles you come to the junction with Road 13S26, where you turn north, toward Kennedy Meadow. This dirt road is generally suitable for two-wheel-drive vehicles, though there may be times when four-wheel drive is necessary.

At a total of 12.3 miles, 13S26 turns into 13S05, though the junction is not marked.

As you approach Evans Meadow, you begin to see wood shacks, large sequoia stumps, and other evidence of Camp Seven, a logging camp of the Hume-Bennett Lumber Company, which clearcut much of the Hume Lake area in the early 1900s. This portion of the road is an old railroad bed used by the early loggers to carry timber to the mill at Hume Lake.

At a total of 15.1 miles, the road comes to a dead end barely big enough to turn around in. Be sure to park so you are not blocking the turnaround area. A wooden trail sign marks the trailhead.

The trail descends from the parking area, following the edge of a small meadow for just 200 feet. At an old campsite, you cross the small creek on redwood planks. This is the last water you will see before Boulder Creek, so make sure your water bottle is full.

You now pass through the heart of Evans Grove, following a century-old logging road. The grove was named after John Evans, who lived near the grove for many years and is said to have protected it from fire. The grove has a great number of handsome sequoias, as well as one very large tree, just 220 yards west of the parking area. The tree is 232 feet high, with a perimeter at breast height of 65.7 feet.

It's worth noting that Evans Grove is not within the Monarch Wilderness, and therefore not given the same level of protection as a wilderness area.

At about 1/2 mile you meet the steep, non-maintained trail which descends from Kennedy Meadow.

At about 3/4 miles the trail leaves the edge of Evans Grove, and begins descending steeply toward Boulder Creek, passing through ponderosa pines and white firs. The trail is not well maintained, but it is passable.

It isn't likely that most hikers will want to descend the nearly 3,000 feet to Boulder Creek, but it is certainly worth descending at least part of the way to enjoy the fines views this trail allows. There aren't many trails which display so much diversity of vegetation over such a short distance.

At about 1 mile, elevation 6400 feet, you reach the boundary of the Monarch Wilderness, marked by a wooden sign.

Looking up canyon you soon have views into the steep and rugged Boulder Creek canyon, including some glimpses of large pools and an occasional waterfall. The large drainage to the east is Rattlesnake Creek.

The trail now becomes increasingly steep, entering large patches of manzanita, bear clover, and yucca. This is snake country, so remember to watch your footing.

At about 1 1/2 miles, elevation 6,000 feet, you begin having some wonderful views of the Monarch Divide to the north. The gnarled rock formations in the foreground are known as the Grand Dike.

By 2 miles, elevation 5600 feet, you begin to see a few laurels, live oaks, pinyon pines, as well as California nutmegs, a fairly uncommon tree in the southern Sierra; the nutmegs short, single needles make it look something like a fir. There is also some poison oak here.

The trail now passes through a belt of marble. This is the same marble formation in which Boyden Cave, just a couple miles to the north, is found.

And at 3 miles, elevation 4800 feet, you reach Boulder Creek, in the bottom of a very rugged gorge, surrounded by ponderosa pines and cedars. This is a good area for fishing, but be extremely careful on the slippery rocks, particularly in the spring and early summer when the water level is high.

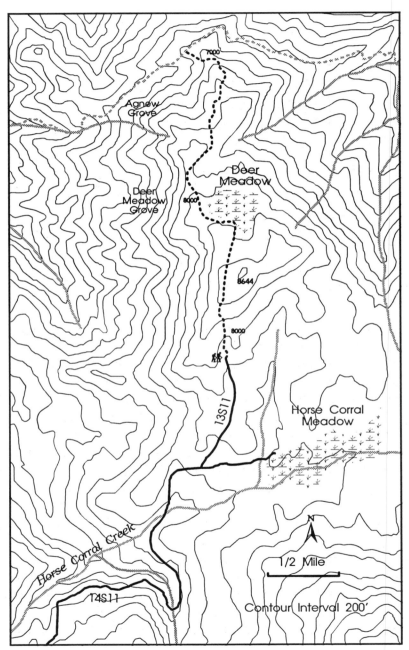

Deer Meadow Trail

DEER MEADOW TRAIL

DISTANCE: 1 1/2 Miles to Deer Meadow; 4 Miles to the Agnew Grove Junction

HIKING TIME: 1 Hour to Deer Meadow; 2 1/2 Hours to the Agnew Grove Junction

STARTING ELEVATION: 7850´

HIGHEST ELEVATION: 8500´

LOWEST ELEVATION: 6800´ at the Agnew Grove Junction

DIFFICULTY: Moderate to Deer Meadow; Strenuous to Points Beyond

USGS MAP: Giant Forest and Tehipite Dome

This seldom-used trail gives access to an extremely rugged area of the Monarch Wilderness. The trail is not maintained, though passable. Most hikers will find the trail as far as Deer Meadow easy and pleasant, but to venture beyond that requires the route-finding skills of experienced hikers.

On the Generals Highway, drive south 6.9 miles from the Grant Grove Visitor Center, or north 4.8 miles from Stony Creek. This brings you to the Big Meadow turnoff (forest service road 14S11), which is marked with a large metal sign that reads, "Big Meadow." Turn east and drive 10.0 miles. Here you turn north on Road 13S11, and drive 0.9 miles to a dead end where the road is blocked by a row of boulders. Be sure to park out of the turnaround area.

(This is a good trail for horses, but you should leave your stock trailer at Horse Corral Meadow, then ride the 1.3 miles to the point described above.)

There is no sign marking the trail; simply follow the logging road uphill, north. If you look to your right, east, you may see part of the original trail in the small drainage just 100 feet away.

This heavily-logged area is covered with stumps, slash, and rutted roads. Obviously, you are not in the wilderness yet.

After about 1/4 mile the road fades, and you may have to look carefully to find the trail. It may be marked with colored flagging. Also, if this area hasn't been clearcut before you hike it, you can look for old blaze marks on the trees.

Though the trail jogs here and there, it generally follows the steepest route up the hill, which gradually becomes more rocky.

At about 1 mile, elevation 8500 feet you reach the top of the ridge. Looking back to the south you can see Marvin Pass, Mitchell Peak, Shell Mountain, and, more to the west, Buck Rock.

From the ridge you can easily climb the rocky knoll to the east, marked 8644 feet on the map. If you take this short detour, you have an outstanding view of the Sierra crest, and of the Great Western Divide.

The trail now descends the north-facing slope, which is cooler and more shaded, and therefore dominated by red firs.

By 1 1/4 miles you begin to see small patches of meadow, and at 1 1/2 miles, elevation 8150 feet, you reach Deer Meadow. This large and beautiful meadow is outside of the Monarch Wilderness, and could one day be vulnerable to the kind of logging you saw on the south side of the ridge.

At the edge of the meadow, and just east of the trail, you pass the remnants of an old log cabin that was once used by ranchers driving their cattle in this country. The cabin's roof has been collapsed by snow, and the walls are beyond repair, but it's view is still as beautiful as ever.

The trail now jogs to the west, following the edge of the meadow, and at about 1 3/4 miles it begins descending more steeply.

At about 2 miles you come to a point where the trail approaches the edge of the canyon, and you can see down into Boulder Creek and its tributaries. By looking carefully to the southwest, you may be able to see a few sequoias in Deer Meadow Grove, perhaps 1,000 feet below you. This small grove, located in a very rugged setting, must be one of the least-visited of all sequoia groves.

At about 2 1/4 miles the trail crosses a small saddle at the point of the ridge. This point marks the boundary of the Monarch Wilderness, though there is no sign. Almost immediately the trail begins dropping even more steeply.

You soon cross a small stringer meadow. Watch for old blaze marks along the faint trail.

There are occasional views across Kings Canyon to Wren Peak, on the Monarch Divide. The trail becomes quite brushy in places.

At about 3 1/2 miles, you cross over the ridge to the west, and follow a very faint trail down the steep slope.

At 4 miles, elevation 6800 feet, the trail passes between a large fir and a large cedar. Here you see a very old, partially destroyed sign which reads, "...Camp Seven... Evans Grove." That non-maintained trail passes through Agnew Grove, and continues down to Boulder Creek; the non-maintained trail you have been following turns to the east and continues to Lightning Creek, and eventually to Cedar Grove.

Only skilled route finders should venture beyond this point.

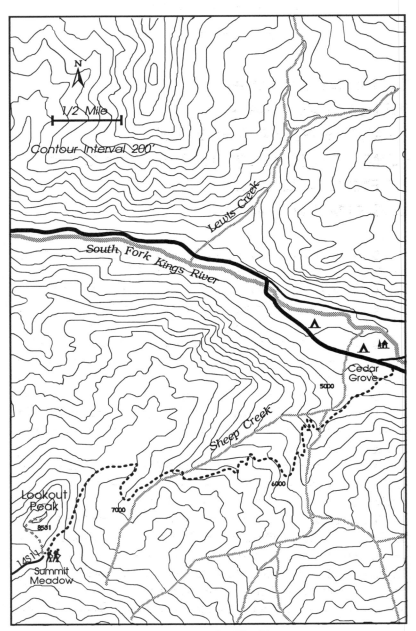

Don   Cecil   Trail

DON CECIL TRAIL

From Summit Meadow

DISTANCE: 5 3/4 Miles
HIKING TIME: 3 Hours
STARTING ELEVATION: 8,000´
LOWEST ELEVATION: 4650´ at Cedar Grove
DIFFICULTY: Moderate
USGS MAP: Marion Peak

Some people say this is the easy way to hike the Don Cecil Trail, because almost every step is downhill. Veteran hikers know, though, that by the end of the day a downhill hike can cause your body a lot more pain than an uphill hike. So let's just say this is the "fast" way to hike the Don Cecil Trail.

If you are planning to have a ride pick you up at Cedar Grove, have them meet you at the amphitheater, next to the ranger station.

Of course it isn't necessary to descend all the way to Cedar Grove. A pleasant, short hike would be to descend only as far as the west fork of Sheep Creek, then return to the parking area at Summit Meadow.

Note that overnight camping is not allowed anywhere along this trail; Sheep Creek is the domestic water source for Cedar Grove, and it's essential that it be kept pure.

To find the Summit Meadow trailhead for the Don Cecil Trail, drive south on the Generals Highway 6.9 miles from the Grant Grove Visitor Center, or drive north on the Generals Highway 4.8 miles from Stony Creek. This brings you to the Big Meadow turnoff (forest service road 14S11), which is marked with a large metal sign that reads, "Big Meadow." Turn east, reset your odometer, and drive 10.4 miles to Horse Corral Meadow; the road forks several times, but it is well marked.

At Horse Corral Meadow (where the last grizzly bear in California was killed by rancher Jesse Agnew in 1922), you continue driving in a northeasterly direction, following the dirt road (14S11). The road is not marked beyond this point; at each junction try to follow the most heavily-used road. After driving a total of 12.5 miles, you begin to have a view of the Monarch Divide to the north, and of Lookout Peak to the northeast.

At 14.1 miles the road crosses the upper end of Summit Meadow. On your left, to the north, is a large, dirt parking area. Be sure to park so that other people can use the turnaround area.

This parking area is on the boundary between Sequoia National Forest and Kings Canyon National Park. Looking to the northeast you can see several signs marking the boundary, as well as the head of the Don Cecil Trail.

From the saddle at the parking area, the trail begins a long, steep traverse into Sheep Creek canyon, passing through white firs, ponderosa pines, and manzanita.

By less than 1/2 mile you begin having some excellent views of the Sierra crest, to the east, as well as of the Cedar Grove area, below. To the north you can see the Monarch Divide; notice on the upper canyons the exceptionally long and graceful glacial moraines.

After 1 mile, elevation 7200 feet, the long traverse ends, as the trail switches back to the south and begins a meandering route to the canyon bottom. You begin seeing a few sugarpines, and looking back to the southwest you can see the summit of Lookout Peak, with its large microwave reflector towers.

At 1 3/4 miles, elevation 6900 feet, you reach the west fork of Sheep Creek. This is a cool and quiet place to rest among the ferns and red willows. The creek usually flows year-round.

The trail now crosses the ridge separating the two main forks of Sheep Creek. Notice some of the very old blaze marks on the trees, an indication of just how old this trail is.

As you begin to descend into the east fork of Sheep Creek, you again have some fine views of the Monarch Divide. The trail soon enters a region of scattered black oaks and kit-kit-dizze, as well as ponderosa pines. And at 4 3/4 miles, elevation 5200 feet, you reach the east fork of Sheep Creek. Here there is a wooden bridge among the alders, as well as a picturesque waterfall. The pools look tempting, but swimming is not allowed.

The trail climbs briefly as you leave the creek drainage, then begins its final descent into Kings Canyon. At about 5 1/2 miles you cross a dirt service road, then pick up the trail again on the other side.

And at 5 3/4 miles, elevation 4650 feet, you reach Highway 180. The amphitheater and Cedar Grove ranger station are just a few hundred feet to the north.

Boole   Tree   Trail

BOOLE TREE TRAIL

DISTANCE: 1 Mile
HIKING TIME: 45 Minutes
STARTING ELEVATION: 6200′
HIGHEST ELEVATION: 6720′
DIFFICULTY: Easy to Moderate
USGS MAP: Tehipite Dome

At one time the Converse Basin Grove was the largest stand of giant sequoias in the world. Between 1897 and 1907 the entire basin, which was then privately owned, was logged. The only sequoia left standing was the Boole Tree, a gnarled and distinctive old specimen which was later shown to be one of the largest sequoias in the world. Ironically, the tree was named after Frank Boole, who supervised the logging operation that destroyed the rest of Converse Basin.

Visiting the Boole Tree today, one hundred years after the surrounding area was heavily logged, you can judge for yourself the lasting effects of a clearcutting operation. Note that although the Boole Tree is not actually in the Monarch Wilderness, it is located just inside the boundary of a special management area where logging activity is to be curtailed in the future.

To find the Boole Tree, starting at the Grant Grove Visitor Center, drive north on Highway 180 4.4 miles. On the west side of the highway, look for forest service road 13S55; it's marked with a sign which reads, "Converse Basin 1 1/2, Stump Meadow 2, Boole Tree Trail 2 1/2." Here you turn left (uphill). Be sure to reset your odometer.

This dirt road is generally suitable for two-wheel-drive passenger vehicles, though there may be times when four-wheel drive is necessary. The road forks a few times, but it is well marked.

The severe soil erosion you see as you pass through this area is one of the long-term, and nearly irreversible, consequences of the heavy logging a century ago.

You pass through Stump Meadow (which looks exactly as its name suggests), and at 2.6 miles you come to a wide turnaround area. On the uphill side of the road is small wooden sign which reads, "Boole Tree 1 Mile."

Though the start of this trail is a bit steep, it's short enough that anybody should be able to complete it if they go slowly.

The trail switchbacks up through manzanita and bear clover, as well as second-growth stands of cedar, ponderosa, and sequoia. Many of the trees here are actually third-generation timber. The first generation was logged between 1897 and 1907, and the second generation was destroyed by the devastating McGee Fire of 1955.

Near the top of the ridge, you pass by a shake pile where a felled sequoia was bucked into lengths, and split into shingles.

You pass through some very tall stands of bitter cherry, with steely-gray bark and oval leaves. It's very unusual to see bitter cherry growing this tall.

As you reach the top of the ridge, elevation 6720 feet, and begin dropping down the north side, you can see the top of the Boole Tree, just a few hundred feet to the north. As you descend the ridge, you see century-old steel cables, and other logging junk, which indicate how close the loggers came to cutting this tree.

Photographs taken in 1903 show how severely this area surrounding the Boole Tree was logged. It's encouraging to see how large the second-growth sequoias have grown in less than 100 years, but its depressing to consider that another 3500 years will be required before they reach the grandeur of the Boole Tree, and other ancient sequoias.

Just before you reach the Boole Tree, you come to an interpretive sign placed there by the Forest Service. Note that the information identifying this as the third largest tree in the world is not correct. Though it is slightly taller than the Grant Tree, and has a ground perimeter greater than the Sherman Tree, in terms of total volume the Boole Tree ranks only eighth largest.

But in terms of character, the Boole Tree is second to none. John Muir called it, quite accurately, "a majestic old scarred monument." Its gnarled branches show that it has known more hardship in its life than most sequoias, and the much smaller second-growth sequoias surrounding the Boole Tree accentuate its great age and nobility.

Little is known about the behind-the-scene politics which led to the saving of the Boole Tree. It has been suggested that the Sanger Lumber Company agreed to spare this one giant in exchange for additional government timber which they could log. As for the naming of the tree, it is said that conservationists fighting to save the tree named it after Frank Boole, the general manager of the Sanger Lumber Company, as a shrewd appeal to his vanity.

Perhaps the time has now come to change the name of this magnificent tree to something more appropriate. Perhaps the "Monarch Tree?"

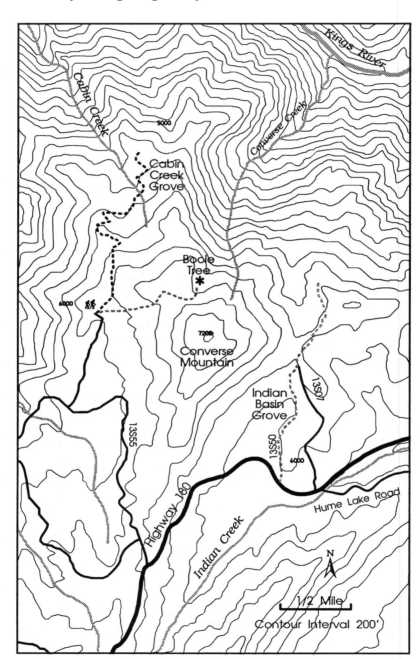

Cabin Creek Grove Trail

CABIN CREEK GROVE TRAIL

DISTANCE: 1 3/4 Miles

HIKING TIME: 1 1/2 Hours

STARTING ELEVATION: 6200'

HIGHEST ELEVATION: 6350'

LOWEST ELEVATION: 5450'

DIFFICULTY: Moderate

USGS MAP: Tehipite Dome

This trail is a delight to hikers who find a special pleasure in seeing sequoia groves that are off the beaten path. Although it's not in the Monarch Wilderness, it's in a special management area which is to be left untouched in the future.

This trail can be hot in midsummer, but it's exceptionally beautiful in the fall when the leaves on the black oaks and bitter cherry change colors.

From the Grant Grove Visitor Center, drive north on Highway 180 4.4 miles. On the west side of the highway, look for forest service road 13S55; it is marked with a sign which reads, "Converse Basin 1 1/2, Stump Meadow 2, Boole Tree Trail 2 1/2." Here you turn left (uphill). Be sure to reset your odometer.

This dirt road is generally suitable for two-wheel-drive vehicles, though there may be times when four-wheel drive is necessary. The road forks a few times, but is well marked.

After passing through Stump Meadow, at 2.6 miles you come to a wide turnaround area. This is the trailhead for the Boole Tree Trail, but there is no trailhead sign marking the Cabin Creek Trail.

Follow Road 13S55 on foot, climbing steeply in almost a straight line to the north. The road, marked by a brown fiberglass post, is a rough and deeply-rutted four-wheel-drive road.

The road passes through kit-kit-dizze, ponderosa pines, and cedars. All the trees here are third-generation timber. The first generation was logged between 1897 and 1907, and the second generation was destroyed by the McGee Fire of 1955.

At about 1/4 mile, elevation 6350 feet, the road ends at the top of the ridge, marked by an old barbed-wire fence.

The trail continues on an old logging road. Actually, this is an old skidway, used by the loggers to move timber to the mill at Converse Basin. Using felled trees as the bed of the skid, and miles of steel cable connected to a steam-powered winch, the loggers dragged the timber out of the forest and to the mill. The wooden skids were oiled to reduce friction, but the heat was still great enough that men had to be posted along the route to extinguish fires.

Though the trail here is not maintained, it is wider and in better condition than many well-groomed trails.

Soon you have spectacular views into lower Kings Canyon, and as far as the San Joaquin Valley to the west. Across the canyon, to the north, is Spanish Mountain.

As the trail descends, you pass through large stands of bitter cherry, some of them more than 20 feet tall. You also see black oaks now, and even a few young, second-growth sequoias.

At 3/4 miles, at a large clearing, the trail narrows again as it turns in a northeasterly direction and begins descending more steeply, following a winding route down the mountain.

Looking to the east you have glimpses of the Converse Mountain Grove of sequoias, near the Boole Tree.

At about 1 1/2 miles, elevation 5800 feet, you reach the edge of the Cabin Creek Grove. Although there has been some light logging in this grove, it escaped the devastating clearcutting that took place in Converse Basin. Perhaps this grove was too remote, and the terrain too rugged.

Most of the cutting in the Cabin Creek Grove was done on windfalls—trees that have fallen naturally. As you pass through the grove, you can still see several post piles and shingle piles left by the loggers a century ago.

As you cross Cabin Creek (a small creek dry by late summer), notice the short corduroy road built by the loggers to get their wagons across the bog.

You pass some very large sequoias which seem, in this remote location, even more noble and stately than other sequoias more easily reached by car.

The trail continues to descend steeply, as it meanders through the grove. There are several spur roads leading to post piles; if you explore these side roads, be sure to keep your bearings; it's easy to get disoriented here.

The trail becomes more faint, until at 1 3/4 miles, elevation 5450 feet, it ends abruptly near the lower edge of the grove. The end of the trail is blocked by an eight-foot-long sequoia log.

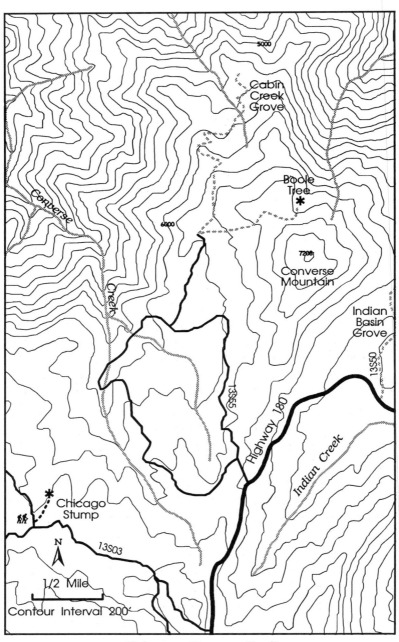

Chicago Stump Trail

CHICAGO STUMP TRAIL

DISTANCE: 1/4 Mile
HIKING TIME: 10 Minutes
STARTING ELEVATION: 6600´
HIGHEST ELEVATION: 6600´
DIFFICULTY: Easy
USGS MAP: Patterson Mountain

This short, easy trail is a quick and stunning education in how the resources of the Converse Basin have been wasted in the last 100 years, and what could have happened to all of Kings Canyon and Sequoia if it hadn't been for the conservation movement of the late 19th Century.

From the Grant Grove Visitor Center, drive north on Highway 180 for 3.1 miles. Turn west on Forest Service Road 13S03, which is marked by a wooden sign, then reset your odometer and follow that dirt road for 1.9 miles, where you come to a junction marked with a sign. Turn north on road 13S65, and at a total of 2.0 miles from Highway 180 you arrive at the trailhead for the Chicago Stump Trail, marked by a large wooden sign on the east side of the road.

This is in the heart of Converse Basin, an area that was clearcut around the turn of the century. Using primitive techniques, the Sanger Lumber Company, and later the Hume-Bennett Lumber Company, devastated what had once been the largest and finest grove of giant sequoias in the world. The greed and waste were so enormous, it has been estimated that as much as 1/2 to 2/3 of the redwood felled was never used.

You may be surprised by how large the new generation of sequoias here are. Sequoias are actually one of the fastest-growing trees in the forest, but it takes hundreds and even thousands of years for them to reach the size of the specimens that were destroyed here in Converse Basin.

Many of the ponderosa pines and sequoias you see growing here are actually third-generation timber. The second-generation was destroyed by the terrible McGee Fire of 1955. That fire was started in the foothills, on the Friday before Labor Day weekend, by a group of ranchers burning brush to improve grazing conditions. At one point the fire spread 3 miles in just 38 minutes. When the fire was finally stopped, two weeks later in the Kings River Canyon, it had blackened 17,580 acres and destroyed enough timber to build 24,000 homes. A pile of sawdust at the old Abbott Mill site smoldered for a year.

After a brief stroll, you arrive at the massive, blackened Chicago Stump. The stump has a perimeter at breast height of nearly 80 feet, which would rank it among the world's largest sequoias if it were still standing. At one time it was known as the General Noble Tree, but it was felled by an entrepreneur in 1892 so that a reassembled cross section of the the tree could be exhibited at the Chicago World's Fair. An interpretive sign, with photos, explains how that foolish act was accomplished.

After the world's fair, the section of the Noble Tree was sent to Washington, D.C., where it was displayed in front of the Department of Agriculture for 30 years. It was then dismantled and shipped to Arlington experimental farms, where it eventually disappeared.

At one time there had been a ladder leading to the top of the Chicago Stump, but the stump was badly burned in the McGee Fire, and the ladder was never replaced.

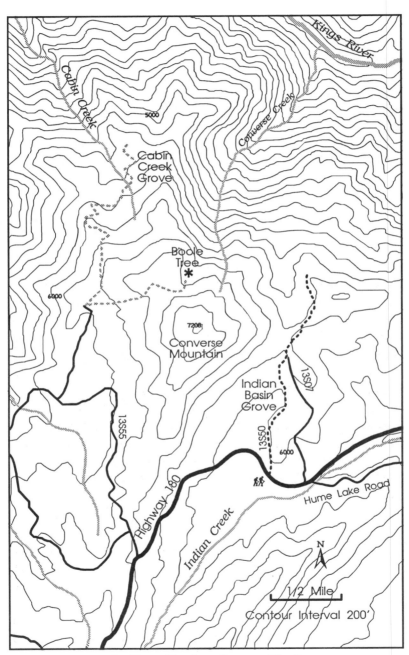

Indian Basin Grove Trail

INDIAN BASIN GROVE TRAIL

DISTANCE: 1 3/4 Miles
HIKING TIME: 1 Hour
STARTING ELEVATION: 5900´
HIGHEST ELEVATION: 6250´
DIFFICULTY: Easy
USGS MAP: Tehipite Dome

Many hikers may not like the fact that the first half of this trail follows a dirt road, and they will probably not appreciate the fact that the Indian Basin Grove of sequoias, which this trail passes through, was heavily logged nearly a hundred years ago. But on the positive side, the dirt road is closed to public traffic, and where the road ends, the wilderness boundary begins. It's also interesting and encouraging to observe how a second growth of young sequoias is replacing the logged-out trees.

Although this trail can be hot in summer, it's beautiful in the fall, and it makes a fine winter ski trail.

The trail begins on Highway 180, 5.6 miles northeast of the Grant Grove Visitor Center, or 0.4 miles west of the entrance to Princess Campground. Here you find forest service road 13S50, marked by a brown fiberglass post. The road is usually locked. Park in the small turnout just west of the road; do not park in the dirt road itself.

Begin by hiking up road 13S50, in a northerly direction, climbing moderately through ponderosa pines and cedars.

At about 1/4 mile you begin to see some medium-size sequoia stumps. The Indian Basin Grove received its name when Indians gathered here to trade with early loggers. The grove was heavily logged during the 1890s, when this land was in private hands. All of the large sequoias were taken, though you can now see some second-generation sequoias about 30 inches in diameter which have grown back. Although this and many other sequoia groves are now within Sequoia National Forest, where intense logging activity is taking place, the current forest service policy is that no commercial logging will occur within the boundaries of the sequoia groves. It remains to be seen whether or not that policy, which doesn't have the weight of law, can survive the intense political pressure to continue logging. If it does, perhaps in a thousand years or so some of these young sequoias will have reached the size of their parent trees.

By 1/2 mile, looking to the southeast, you have glimpses of Hume Lake, named for Thomas Hume, a multi-millionaire timber baron from Michigan. Hume, with a local investor named Ira Bennett, bought the ailing Sanger Lumber Company, which had gone bankrupt after clearcutting the world's largest stand of giant sequoias at Converse Basin. The Hume-Bennett Lumber Company acquired new timber lands to the west of Converse Basin, dammed Tenmile Creek, thus creating Hume Lake, built a mill and a 54-mile flume to deliver the lumber to Sanger, then proceeded to clearcut the Hume Lake Basin.

The Hume Lake area was nearly included in Sequoia National Park in 1919, but when the director of the National Park Service, Stephen Mather, toured the area he decided it was too damaged to be part of the park. The land was bought by the government in 1935, and became part of Sequoia National Forest.

At about 1 mile you meet road 13S07, which returns to Highway 180 just across from the Hume Lake Road.

Continuing to the north, at about 1 1/4 miles, elevation 6250 feet, you reach the ridge top near a small campsite. This ridge, which is a shoulder of Converse Mountain to the west, marks the boundary of a special management area where logging activity is to be curtailed in the future.

The road jogs to the east, and after 300 yards you leave the road to join the old trail, which now turns to the north. The trail is not marked by a sign, but it is broad and not easy to miss. It begins in a patch of manzanita and buck brush.

The trail rises and falls slightly, as you continue to the north, passing through black oaks and cedars.

This trail is part of an old skidway, used by loggers to move timber to the mill at Hume Lake Basin. Using felled trees as the bed of the skid, and miles of steel cable connected to a steam-powered winch, the loggers dragged the timber out of the forest and to the mill. The wooden skids were oiled to reduce friction, but the heat was still great enough that men had to be posted along the route to extinguish fires. After the marketable timber was removed from an area, the skids were abandoned, and the logs went to waste.

Looking a few hundred yards to the west, you can see several second-growth sequoias in the Converse Mountain Grove. They are easily recognized from a distance by their symmetrical, conical shape. There are also a few large sequoias there which escaped the logging.

At about 1 1/2 miles, the trail climbs steeply for just a short ways, then descends steeply.

At about 1 3/4 miles, elevation 6100 feet, the trail ends abruptly on a point overlooking Kings Canyon. Though you can't see Kings River at the bottom of the canyon, some 4,000 feet below, if you listen carefully you can probably hear its distant roar.

The massive, rugged mountain to the north is Spanish Mountain. To the northeast you can see up the Middle Fork of the Kings. To the east you can see the Monarch Divide, and to the distant east you can see the crest of the Sierra Nevada.

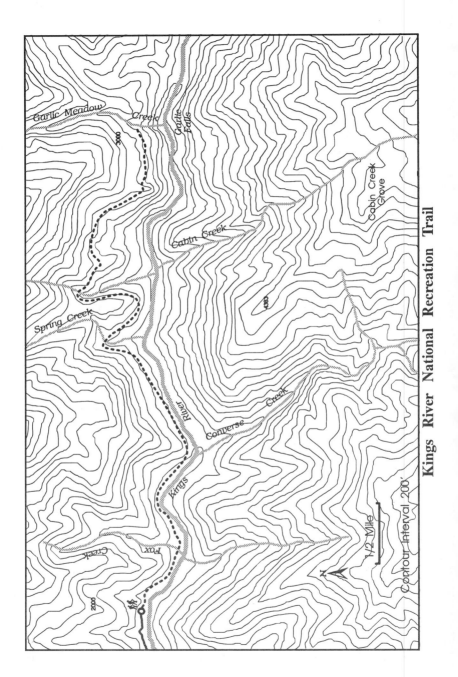

Kings River National Recreation Trail

KINGS RIVER
NATIONAL RECREATION TRAIL

DISTANCE: 3 Miles to Spring Creek; 5 Miles to Garlic Meadow Creek

HIKING TIME: 2 Hours to Spring Creek; 4 Hours to Garlic Meadow Creek

STARTING ELEVATION: 1650´

HIGHEST ELEVATION: 1800´ at Spring Creek; 2800´ at Garlic Spur

DIFFICULTY: Easy to Spring Creek; Strenuous to Garlic Meadow Creek

USGS MAP: Patterson Mountain and Tehipite Dome

This trailhead is difficult to reach, requiring a drive of nearly 30 miles on windy, dirt roads. But if you've already completed several of the hikes in upper Kings Canyon, you're no doubt curious about what the lower canyon looks like. This is one of the few trails that can get you there. It follows the very belly of the lower canyon, and in terms of wild beauty it is a match for by any day-hiking trail in the southern Sierra.

Like all of the lower foothills, this area is quite hot in the summer. Plan this hike for the spring, when the wild poppies are in bloom, or for the fall. Winter is also good, if the road conditions allow access.

From Highway 180, about 6 miles below the Big Stump entrance station, turn north on forest service road 12S01. The road is marked by a large brown sign which reads, "McKenzie Heliport, Delilah Lookout, Camp 4 1/2." Follow road 12S01 to the Kings River at Camp 4 1/2. Although the road forks several times, it is well marked. This dirt road is suitable for two-wheel-drive vehicles, though there may be times when four-wheel drive is necessary. Plan on about a one-hour drive from Highway 180 to the Kings River.

At 17.5 miles you reach the Kings River. Here you turn west, and at 20 miles you reach Rodgers Crossing. Cross the bridge and turn east, following the sign to "Kings River Trail." At a total of 27 miles, the road ends. Look for the trailhead at the east end of the parking area.

For the first few hundred feet, the trail follows a dirt road which leads to a mine in Fox Canyon. But the trail soon leaves the road and follows a route just above the Kings River, passing through scattered live oaks, ponderosa pines, and sycamores.

Here, deep in the bottom of the canyon, the river is broad and powerful, alternating between turbulent rapids and massive pools. The wild Kings is larger than the Kern and Kaweah Rivers in Sequoia, and in fact in the southern Sierra it is only rivaled by the San Joaquin, which unfortunately has been dammed almost its entire length. A proposed dam at Rodgers Crossing would have flooded 11 miles of this lower canyon, but that proposal, which was favored by corporate farmers on the west side of the San Joaquin Valley, was put to rest in 1989 when this was officially designated a special management area.

The trail climbs very gently now. Looking to the south, across the river, is an unnamed creek and canyon, both rugged and inaccessible. In the spring you can see a large waterfall about halfway up that creek.

Note that all along this trail poison oak grows with exceptional health and vigor, though it has mostly been pruned away from the trail itself. Look for the shiny oak-like leaves; in the fall, after the leaves have fallen, look for the white berries.

After about 3/4 miles, the trail approaches the river at a large flat. There are excellent fishing spots here, and in fact all along this trail.

By 1 1/2 miles you have a view across the river and up Converse Creek and its extremely steep and rugged canyon. As you approach the point where Converse Creek flows into the Kings, if you look carefully on the south side of the river, you can see a young sequoia growing on a gravel bed above the river. (Don't confuse it with the cedars which also grow nearby.) This young sequoia most likely washed down as a young seedling during a flood, and then took root. Sequoias grow surprisingly well at these lower elevations as long as they have a reliable source of water.

At about 2 miles the river and trail make a sweeping bend, after which you can see far up canyon to Junction Ridge and the Monarch Divide.

At about 3 miles, elevation 1800 feet, you reach Spring Creek, where there is a short but very pretty waterfall above the trail. There are also fine pools here along the creek, as well as good places to rest.

From Spring Creek the trail climbs steeply as it leaves the river and ascends Garlic Spur, a long ridge which ends abruptly at the canyon's edge. As you stop to catch your breath, look down on the gravel beds along the river, where you can see large redwood logs which have washed down over the years.

Along the trail above Spring Creek you might find black flakes of obsidian, which indicate that this trail was used as a migration and trading route by the Monache Indians. The nearest source of obsidian is the Mono Craters, on the east side of the Sierra and more than 100 miles to the north.

The trail passes through yucca plants, which look like bluish-green balls of spikes. In the spring they send out long, pointed stalks with cream-colored flowers. The Indians baked yucca stalks and ate it like squash.

You also find buckeye trees along the trail here, with bright green leaves and long cream-colored flower clusters. In the summer buckeyes usually go dormant; their leaves turn brown and eventually drop; by late fall only the large seed pods remain on the branches, looking like Christmas decorations.

At about 3 3/4 miles you cross an unnamed creek. Directly across the river you see Cabin Creek, which has a fine grove of sequoias at its head.

The trail continues climbing steeply, and crosses a series of small unnamed creeks. Each of these creeks has a lush stand of stinging nettle, also known as "hoary nettle." If you aren't familiar with this troublesome 3-foot to 6-foot plant, the stalks are covered with tiny hairs which are very painful to the touch and can leave a sting which lasts for several hours. (The sting is caused by an injection of formic acid.)

Almost as an apology for the stinging nettle, these same creeks also shelter dense thickets of spice bush, one of the prettiest shrubs in the Sierra. It has brilliant green leaves and red flower clusters.

At about 4 1/2 miles, elevation 2800 feet, you reach the top of Garlic Spur, where you have a view far up the Kings River to the crest of the Sierra. More in the forefront, you can see Windy Cliffs.

The trail now contours around Garlic Spur, then descends through thick stands of yerba santa, to Garlic Meadow Creek, distance 5 miles, elevation 2600 feet. This is a fairly large creek, heavily wooded with alders. A short ways upstream there are small pools and flat areas to rest. Use extreme caution here, particularly in the spring and early summer when the water level is high.

The trail is not maintained beyond Garlic Meadow Creek, though the Forest Service is considering building a new trail that will continue up canyon.

Caution: On the Tehipite Dome Quadrangle, and other maps, you see Garlic Falls located just downstream from the point where this trail reaches the creek. Do not try to hike down the creek to Garlic Falls! The creek is extremely steep and rugged, and the route is choked with poison oak. Garlic Falls can be safely viewed from the Yucca Point Overlook, on Highway 180.

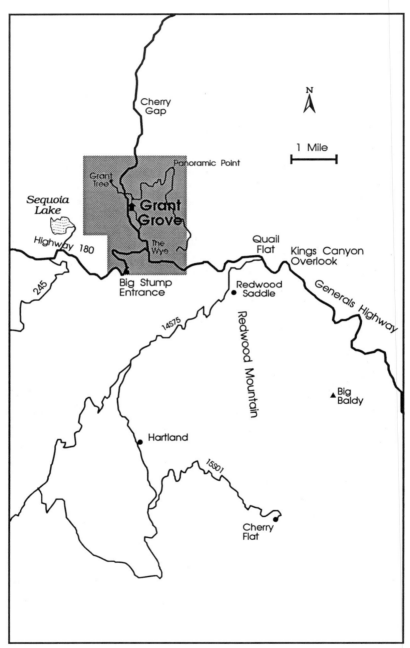

Grant   Grove

INTRODUCTION
TO
GRANT GROVE

Grant Grove was established as a national park in 1890, with the same legislation that established Sequoia National Park. Originally, it was just a four-section block of land—2,400 acres—surrounding the General Grant Tree. When the huge Kings Canyon National Park was established, in 1940, Grant Grove was incorporated into the new park. But the boundaries of the original park are still roughly marked by the North Boundary Trail, the South Boundary Trail, the Sunset Trail, and the Park Ridge Trail, which were fire breaks and fire access roads protecting the small park.

Grant Grove lies along what was once an Indian migration route from the lower foothills to the high country. That route came up Mill Flat Creek, passed through what is now Azalea Campground, over Panoramic Point, Burton Pass, and then down Sheep Creek into Cedar Grove. Judging by the mortar holes left by the Indians near Azalea Campground, they spent a good deal of time in this area. The temperature is moderate most of the year; there are lots of black oaks to provide acorns in the fall, and even today deer and other game are plentiful.

The General Grant Tree is still the center of attention in the Grant Grove area. In terms of total volume, it's the third largest tree in the world, and by any standard it is one of the most beautiful giant sequoias still standing.

Aside from the Grant Tree itself, one of the major attractions at Grant Grove is the display of wild azaleas when they are in bloom—between May and August. Sequoia Creek, which is accessible from the Azalea Trail and the South Boundary Trail, is one of the best places to enjoy the azaleas.

Ella and Viola Falls, both small but pretty waterfalls, are well worth a hiker's time. They can be seen from the Sunset, Hitchcock Meadow, and South Boundary Trails.

There are several historic logging sites in the Grant Grove area that are accessible by trails in this guidebook, including the Big Stump Loop, the Hitchcock Meadow Trail, the North Grove Loop, and the Sunset Trail. There is also one very important logging site—the old town of Millwood—which is outside of the National Park, and best reached by road. Hikers who are interested in the history of the Grant Grove area may want to visit that site, so directions to it are given here:

To reach Millwood by car, from the Big Stump entrance station, drive west on Highway 180 for 2.2 miles; turn north at the Sequoia Lake turnoff, and immediately turn northwest on Forest Service road 13S97; then drive 2.3 miles to the confluence of Mill Flat Creek and Abbott Creek. Except for a badly eroded hillside, there is almost no physical evidence of Millwood still in existence. Established in 1891, the town grew to accommodate perhaps 2,000 employees of the Sanger Lumber Company, and their families. The town included a hotel, post office, general store, butcher shop, blacksmith, doctor's office, barns, cookhouse, and employee shacks. Apparently there was no church, though the town is known to have had an active red-light district.

And finally, for those visitors who may have visited the Grant Grove area some years ago, the old market and lodge at Wilsonia were closed in 1991. Now the only grocery store is at Grant Grove Village, where there is also a lodge, restaurant, bar, gift shop, gas station, post office, and park service visitor center—but no red-light district.

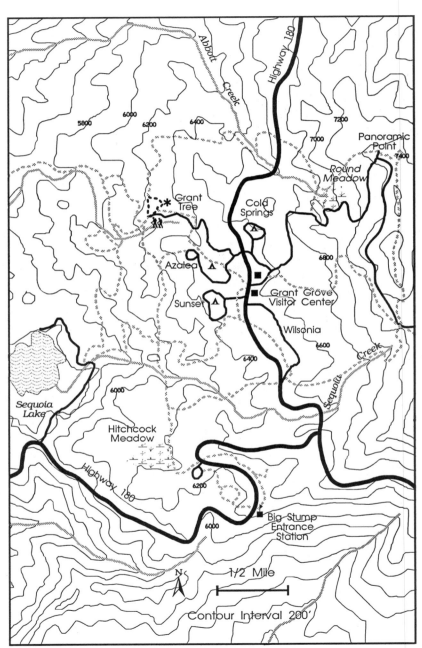

General Grant Tree Loop

GENERAL GRANT TREE LOOP

DISTANCE: 1/2 Mile
HIKING TIME: 30 Minutes
STARTING ELEVATION: 6320´
HIGHEST ELEVATION: 6400´
DIFFICULTY: Easy
USGS MAP: Giant Forest

This short trail is very popular in the summer, and is not the place to go if you're looking for seclusion; but it does feature some of the largest sequoias in the world, as well as the nation's Christmas Tree, the Grant Tree.

From the Grant Grove Visitor Center, drive north on Highway 180 for 0.2 miles; turn left (west) and drive 0.7 miles on the road to the General Grant Tree parking area. The paved trail begins at the north end of the parking area.

A short climb brings you to the Fallen Monarch, a fire-hollowed sequoia which provides an unusual shelter. Thomas and Israel Gamlin, early settlers in this area, used the Fallen Monarch as a cabin, and later as a saloon. When Grant Grove became a national park, in 1890, the U.S. Cavalry, which provided the first park rangers, used the Fallen Monarch as a stable for their horses. In bad weather they sheltered as many as 32 horses here.

Continuing up the trail, you come to the General Grant Tree. Though its diameter at breast height is greater than any sequoia, in terms of total volume it ranks third, behind the Sherman Tree and the Washington Tree, both in Giant Forest.

The Grant Tree was discovered in 1862 by Joseph Hardin Thomas, and named after General Ulysses S. Grant in 1867.

For those foreign visitors who might not be familiar with American history, or for those American visitors who might not be familiar with American history, Ulysses S. Grant was the general in command of the Union army during the Civil War. He later went on to become a notorious alcoholic, and one of the most corrupt U.S. presidents in American history.

In 1926 the Grant Tree was designated the nation's Christmas Tree, and each year there is a Christmas service held at its base. Some estimates put the tree's age at 3500 years, or about 1500 years older than the celebration of Christmas itself.

A little farther around the loop, you come to the Gamlin Cabin, built in 1872 by Israel Gamlin, a homesteader. In later years, this simple but sturdy structure became the first park ranger station at Grant Grove.

As you finish the loop, you pass by the Centennial Stump. This sequoia was felled in 1872, after taking two men nine days to chop and saw through its twenty-four-foot base. A sixteen-foot section of the tree was sent to the nation's centennial celebration, held in Philadelphia in 1876. Skeptical spectators at the celebration refused to believe it was one tree, insisting that it must be several trees pieced together. It probably would not have eased their skepticism any if they were told this was only an average-size sequoia—others from this same grove are much larger.

Later, the Centennial Stump became known as the "School Stump" because mothers and children from the nearby logging camps held Sunday School services here. Fathers, of course, were up at the Fallen Monarch Saloon holding their own Sunday services.

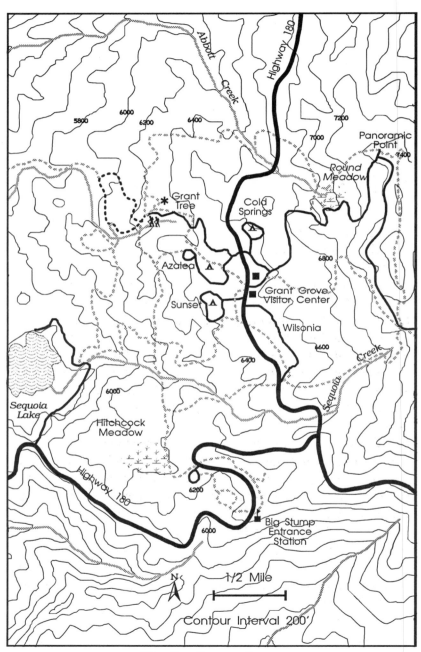

North Grove Loop

NORTH GROVE LOOP

DISTANCE: 2 Miles

HIKING TIME: 1 1/2 Hours

STARTING ELEVATION: 6350′

LOWEST ELEVATION: 5950′

DIFFICULTY: Easy

USGS MAP: Giant Forest and Tehipite Dome

This really isn't a trail, it's a fire road closed to private vehicles. Still, it's an opportunity to see a quiet corner of the Grant Grove of sequoias.

From the Grant Grove Visitor Center, drive north on Highway 180 for 0.2 miles; turn left (west) and drive 0.7 miles on the road to the General Grant Tree parking area. Proceed to the far west end (the lower end) of the parking area, where you see a locked gate and a sign which reads "North Grove Loop."

The trail follows the fire road downhill, passing through a stand of large sequoias. At less than 1/4 mile, you come to a junction with the Dead Giant Loop. Take the upper fork, to the west.

The trail now descends moderately, passing through white firs, ponderosa and sugarpines, as well as a few large sequoias.

As the trail passes through a small meadow, notice the large sequoia stumps. This area was partially logged prior to the establishment of Grant Grove National Park, in 1890.

Notice also the large burn scars at the base of several live sequoias. The thick bark of the sequoias is very fire resistant, but once fire has managed to get into the wood of the tree, the bark works to the tree's disadvantage, acting as insulation and increasing the heat of the fire. In this way, fires hollow out large chambers, known as "cat faces," at the base of almost all large sequoias.

At about 1 mile, elevation 5950 feet, you come to the lowest point on this loop. Here, on the west side of the trail, you see an old wooden sign which reads "Millwood Fire Road." This is an interesting detour which, if you choose to take it, will add about 1 mile to your hike.

(Millwood Road: The old road quickly narrows into a trail, as it descends through a group of large sequoias. Though this road hardly looks used now, around the turn of the century it was a major route from the park to the logging town of Millwood.

The trail crosses the park boundary, marked by a row of old fence posts, and enters Sequoia National Forest. As the trail descends more steeply, following the route of Mill Flat Creek, you see even more large sequoia stumps.

At about 1/2 mile, at an open flat, you meet forest service road 13S63. If you would like to visit the site of Millwood, which is still 2 1/4 miles below this point, it is probably best to get there by car. See the Introduction to Grant Grove for directions to Millwood.)

Continuing on the North Grove Loop, from the Millwood Road junction, you now turn in a southerly direction and begin climbing fairly steeply.

In recent years the Park Service has been conducting prescribed burns in the North Grove area to reduce the accumulation of forest litter and to create a healthier forest. In some burned areas you see an open forest floor, with young pine and sequoia seedlings; in unburned areas you see impassable snarls of dead trees and limbs where plant regeneration can't take place.

At 1 1/2 miles, elevation 6080 feet, you come to a junction with the Dead Giant Loop and the Sunset Trail. Here you continue uphill, to the east.

At 1 3/4 miles you complete the loop, and continue east 1/4 mile to the parking area.

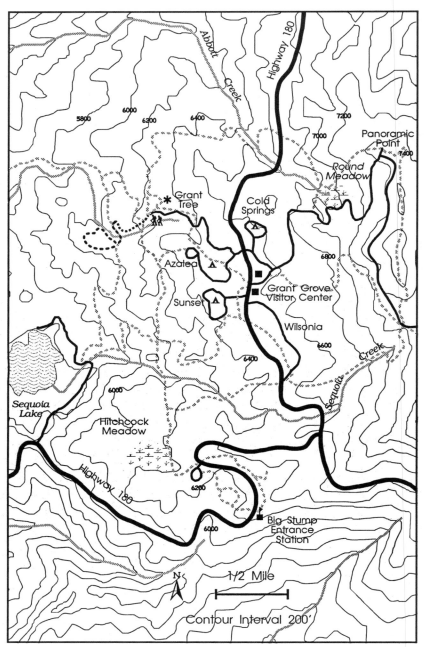

Dead Giant Loop

DEAD GIANT LOOP

DISTANCE: 2 1/4 Miles

HIKING TIME: 1 1/2 Hours

STARTING ELEVATION: 6350´

LOWEST ELEVATION: 6100´

DIFFICULTY: Easy

USGS MAP: Giant Forest

This short trail offers an excellent view of historical Sequoia Lake, the center of logging activity in this area during the 1890s.

From the Grant Grove Visitor Center, drive north on Highway 180 for 0.2 miles; turn left (west) and drive 0.7 miles on the road to the General Grant Tree parking area. Proceed to the lower end of the parking area, where you see a locked gate and a sign which reads "North Grove Loop." The Dead Giant Loop and the North Grove Loop share the first 3/4 miles.

The trail follows the fire road downhill. At less than 1/4 mile, you come to a junction of the North Grove Loop. Take the lower trail, to the southwest.

About 1/2 mile brings you to a second junction, where you leave the North Grove Loop and continue to the south.

The trail now circles a lush meadow surrounded by medium-size sequoias, and at 3/4 miles, elevation 6100 feet, you come to junction marked by a sign which reads "Dead Giant." Here you turn west, and in a short ways reach the Dead Giant.

With a perimeter at breast height of 61 feet, the Dead Giant qualifies as one of the very large sequoias. As you can see by the remnants of bark which still cling to the trunk, it hasn't been dead for very many years. On several of the buttresses, just 2 or 3 feet off the ground, you can see axe marks, as if loggers had been preparing a typical scaffolding in preparation to fell the tree. Why the job wasn't completed, nobody knows.

The trail now circles around the knoll, climbing slightly. And at about 1 1/4 miles, elevation 6,000 feet, you come to the Sequoia Lake Overlook. The best view point is about 300 feet south of the loop.

In August of 1889, the Kings River Lumber Company built a dam on Mill Flat Creek, creating Sequoia Lake. The water was diverted into a wooden flume 54 miles long, which ended at the town of Sanger. During the next several years, millions of board feet of lumber were cut and milled in this basin, then sent down the flume to be finished at the planing mill in Sanger.

After all the effort of building the lake and flume, the lumber company went bankrupt, and was sold. To recover their investment, the new owners moved the entire operation over the ridge to Converse Basin, where they set about clearcutting the world's largest stand of giant sequoias.

Continuing around the loop, at 1 1/2 miles you return to the junction at elevation 6100 feet. You now hike back to General Grant Tree parking area by the same route as you came.

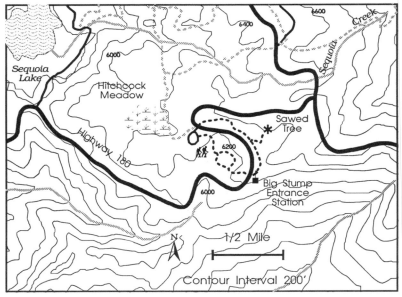

Big   Stump   Loop

BIG STUMP LOOP

DISTANCE: 1 Mile
HIKING TIME: 1 Hour
STARTING ELEVATION: 6260´
HIGHEST ELEVATION: 6400´ at the Sawed Tree
DIFFICULTY: Easy
USGS MAP: Giant Forest

Between 1883 and 1889, much of the Big Stump Grove was gutted by loggers. At that time almost everybody considered this country's timber resources to be unlimited, put here by god for man to use in any way he saw fit. It took the destruction of this grove, and of the nearby Converse Basin Grove, to convince Americans how precious and rare giant sequoias really are.

Even more disheartening than the original destruction of this grove is to see how little the passage of one hundred years has done to heal the damage. For all their massive size and stubborn resistance to disease, giant sequoias and their native domain are very fragile.

Begin at the Big Stump parking area. From the Grant Grove Visitor Center, drive south on Highway 180 1.4 miles to the Wye (the intersection of Highway 180 and the Generals Highway), turn west (right) on 180 and drive 1.0 miles to the Big Stump parking area. Look for the trailhead near the restroom, at the south end of the parking area.

The trail begins downhill, and in just 200 feet you come to the Resurrection Tree, a gnarled sequoia which lost its top to lightning but is now making a hardy effort to grow a new one. Except for human meddling, lightning is probably the biggest threat to large sequoias. It's rare to find an old sequoia that doesn't show the damage from at least one lightning bolt. Even worse than the initial strike, sometimes the fire started by the strike will burn inside the tree for weeks, hollowing out huge blackened chambers.

The trail meanders downhill, passing several large sequoia stumps, as well as some cut logs which were used for making shake shingles. The wood of giant sequoias is too brittle for most construction purposes; many of the sequoias were felled, bucked into lengths, then split into fence posts, grape stakes, and roof shingles.

Less then 1/4 mile down the trail, you come to a fork. This is a loop within a loop, encircling the site of the old Smith Comstock Mill. It doesn't matter which fork you take, but for now take the right fork and continue south.

Soon you come to the Shattered Giant, a felled sequoia that broke in so many places it was mostly unusable. Like all sequoia logging operations of the 19th Century, the waste here was enormous. A team of sawyers might work for a week to fell a big tree, only to have it shatter into pieces when it hit the ground. But labor was cheap, and plenty more sequoias were available, so the loggers simply went on to the next tree rather than salvage their last mistake.

You can now see the meadow which was the site of the Smith Comstock Mill. Besides many stumps and shattered logs, you see several orange-red piles of sawdust left by the mill. Even in the form of sawdust, sequoia wood rots very little in a hundred years.

Continue circling the meadow, staying to your left at the next junction, until you come to the site of the Featherbed, marked by a metal sign. In an attempt to cushion the fall of the sequoias, the loggers would sometimes dig trenches where they hoped the trees would land, then line the trenches with slash, or branches cut from other trees.

You pass a wooden sign marking the site of the Smith Comstock Mill, as well as a sign marking two sequoias planted by a logger of that era. As you can see by the considerable size of these trees, young sequoias grow quite rapidly.

And a short distance farther brings you to the Burnt Monarch, a dead standing sequoia also known as "Old Adam" because the loggers considered it to be the patriarch of this grove. When it was alive, this tree may have been the patriarch of all sequoias. At breast height it measures 97.8 feet in circumference, making it larger than the General Sherman Tree, which is the largest living sequoia.

Surrounding the Burnt Monarch is an exceptionally beautiful group of azaleas; if you happen to be here in the early summer, when the azalea shrubs are in bloom, you'll see a fine flower display.

You now backtrack about 1/8 mile to the last fork you passed, and continue hiking southwest to the Mark Twain Stump. This tree was cut in 1891, two years after the Smith Comstock Mill had stopped operating here. The reason? As foolish as it might seem now, this 1500-year-old sequoia was cut down so the American Museum of Natural History, in New York, could have a slice to put on display.

(Keep in mind that although the giant sequoias inside the boundaries of General Grant National Park were protected as early as 1890, this particular area wasn't included in the park until 1965.)

After it was felled, the Mark Twain Tree was bucked, then a section was split into twelve pieces, which were floated down the Sanger Lumber Company's Flume to the San Joaquin Valley. There Collis B. Huntington, president of the Southern Pacific Railroad, and a shrewd promoter, shipped the pieces free of charge to New York, where they were reassembled at the museum.

You now climb a short distance to the Big Stump entrance station, total distance 1/2 mile, elevation 6240 feet. Cross Highway 180 on the painted crosswalk, and pick up the trail again on the east side.

The trail climbs gradually, crossing a small creek, and passing several more sequoia stumps.

At about 3/4 miles you come to a sign marking a short, uphill detour to the Sawed Tree. As you can see, an undercut—the first cut loggers make in a tree—was made here. The undercut is supposed to face in the direction the logger wants the tree to fall—downhill in this case—but the lean of this tree is uphill, which means the tree never could have fallen where the loggers intended it to go. Once the loggers had sobered up enough to realize their mistake, they simply abandoned the tree. Amazingly, this tree survived their butchered felling job.

Continuing along the Big Stump Loop, at 1 mile you again reach Highway 180. Follow the culvert tunnel under the highway and back to the parking area.

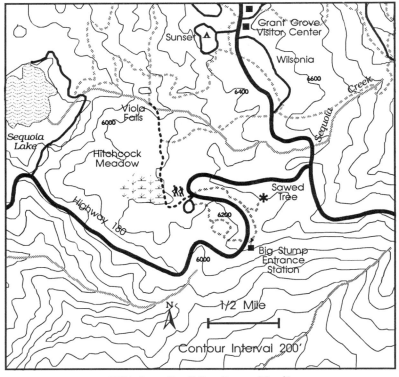

Hitchcock   Meadow   Trail

HITCHCOCK MEADOW TRAIL

Big Stump to Viola Falls

DISTANCE: 1 3/4 Miles
HIKING TIME: 1 Hour
STARTING ELEVATION: 6260´
LOWEST ELEVATION: 5920´ at Sequoia Creek
DIFFICULTY: Easy
USGS MAP: Giant Forest

This trail passes through a historic logging area before arriving at very pretty Viola Falls, which is the perfect site for an afternoon picnic.

From the Grant Grove Visitor Center, drive south on Highway 180 1.4 miles to the Wye (the intersection of Highway 180 and the Generals Highway), turn west on 180 and drive 1.0 miles to the Big Stump parking area.

The trailhead, marked by a large sign, is at the north end of the parking area, near the tunnel. (Disregard the distances given on the trailhead sign, which are confusing at best.)

The trail descends fairly steeply, soon leaving Kings Canyon National Park and entering Sequoia National Forest.

You pass through an area that was logged very heavily by the Smith Comstock Mill between 1883 and 1889. Amazingly, some of the sequoia stumps still haven't shed their bark. On several of the stumps you can see the notches cut by the loggers to support the wooden scaffolding which allowed them to cut above the tree's butt swell.

At 3/4 miles, elevation 6150 feet, you arrive at Hitchcock Meadow, a medium-size meadow with large sequoia stumps surrounding it. Notice the young, one-hundred-year-old sequoias which are beginning to replace the parent trees that were logged here.

The trail now rises and falls only slightly, as it follows a long stringer meadow with thick clumps of red willow.

At 1 1/4 miles, elevation 6150 feet, you come to a junction with the South Boundary Trail, which is described in the chapter of that name.

Climbing just a bit more, to elevation 6200 feet, you reach the top of the ridge, where you leave Sequoia National Forest and enter Kings Canyon National Park.

The trail descends steeply now, following short switchbacks, and at 1 3/4 miles, elevation 5920 feet, you come to Sequoia Creek. This is a pretty spot, with ferns, dogwoods and a few giant sequoias. If you cross the creek on a culvert bridge, just north of the creek you see a sign which directs you to Viola Falls, just a few hundred feet downstream.

The falls itself is actually a series of short steps which, when the water level is high, join into one large falls. There are flat places above the falls where you can rest or have lunch.

Below Viola Falls, the canyon is very steep and treacherous. Don't venture down canyon.

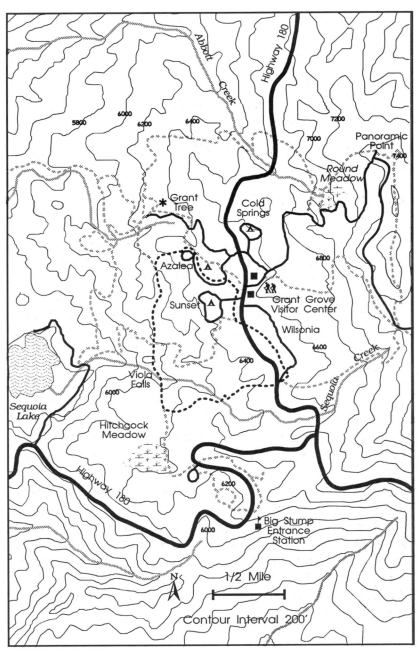

South Boundary Trail

SOUTH BOUNDARY TRAIL

DISTANCE: 4 3/4 Miles (A Loop Trail)

HIKING TIME: 3 Hours

STARTING ELEVATION: 6589´ at Grant Grove
Visitor Center

LOWEST ELEVATION: 5920´ at Sequoia Creek

DIFFICULTY: Moderate

USGS MAP: Giant Forest

At one time this trail was known by the more intriguing name, "The Dark Canyon Trail." Though it's used far less than several other trails in the area, it's really one of the most beautiful and interesting trail's Grant Grove has to offer.

It's possible to hike this as a one-way trail, from Azalea Campground to the Grant Grove Visitor Center, but hiking it as a loop saves you the inconvenience of shuttling cars.

Beginning at the Grant Grove Visitor Center, cross Highway 180 at the painted crosswalk. Descend the trail and stairs to the amphitheater, then turn north and follow the trail to Azalea Campground, crossing the meadow on a wooden footbridge. From the bulletin board in the campground, follow the main road to the far northwest end of the campground. Just south of campsite #110, you see a small turnout and a wooden sign which reads "S. Boundary Trail." The distance to this point is 3/4 miles, elevation 6500 feet.

The trail descends the ridge, passing through ponderosa and sugarpines, and at less than 1 mile you begin to see the buildings at the Swale Work Center. The Swale Work Center is currently being used as the base camp for the Arrowhead hotshot firefightning crew, which responds to National Park Service wildfires all across the West.

About 300 feet east of Swale, you see a trail junction marked by a small wooden sign which reads "Trail." Here you turn to the south, following a route which passes just above the Swale Work Center.

At the south end of Swale, the trail skirts a small meadow and begins descending gently, passing through a dense forest of white firs, cedars, sugarpines, and a few black oaks.

At about 1 3/4 miles, elevation 6000 feet, you come to a junction with the Sunset Trail. (A 1/2 mile detour, following the Sunset Trail to the west, would bring you to Ella Falls, elevation 5600 feet.) Cross the Sunset Trail, and continue in a southerly direction.

The trail descends mildly until, at 2 miles, elevation 5920 feet, you reach Sequoia Creek, a small but very pretty creek, with ferns, dogwoods, and even a few sequoias growing along its banks. Just north of the creek a wooden trail signs directs you to Viola Falls, which is just a few hundred feet to the west.

The falls itself is actually a series of short steps which, when the water level is high, join into one large falls. Here the water has sculpted gracefully-shaped pools into the granite creek bed. There are flat areas above the falls where you can rest or sun yourself on the rocks.

In August of 1889, Sequoia Creek was dammed at Mill Flat Meadow, about a mile to the west. The water from the newly-formed Sequoia Lake was then used to feed a lumber flume which ran 54 miles to Sanger, on the floor of the San Joaquin Valley. The Kings River Lumber Company logged 19,000,000 board feet of timber in this area, and cut down 8,000 giant sequoias. The milled lumber was sent down the flume to Sanger.

Below Viola Falls, the canyon is very steep and treacherous. Don't venture down canyon.

Continuing on the South Boundary Trail, you now cross Sequoia Creek on a culvert bridge, and begin climbing fairly steeply. Notice the large sequoia stumps from the logging operations which took place here before the establishment of Grant Grove National Park, in 1890.

At about 2 1/4 miles, elevation 6200 feet, you reach the top of the ridge, which happens to be the approximate location of the boundary between Kings Canyon National Park and Sequoia National Forest.

The trail descends slightly, and at 2 1/2 miles you come to a junction near a long stringer meadow. (The trail to the south is the Hitchcock Meadow Trail, and leads 1 1/4 miles to the Big Stump parking area.) The South Boundary Trail turns to the east, following the edge of the long stringer meadow.

You soon pass back into Kings Canyon National Park, and continue climbing fairly steeply, until you reach the top of a ridge at elevation 6320 feet.

The trail contours around the ridge until, at 3 miles, you again reach Sequoia Creek.

There are few places in the southern Sierra where azaleas grow as well as they do along Sequoia Creek, and this section of the creek is no exception. As pretty as they may be, though, azaleas contain a toxin which can cause convulsions and paralysis.

The trail crosses Sequoia Creek on a wooden footbridge, and begins climbing again as it passes among some large, fine sugarpines.

After climbing fairly steeply, the trail meets a dirt service road and turns to the north.

At 3 3/4 miles, elevation 6450 feet, you again reach Highway 180.

Cross the highway and, on the east side, join the Azalea Trail, marked by a wooden sign.

Turning north on the Azalea Trail, you follow a route near the Highway 180. The trail crosses the highway near Sunset Campground, and passes above the amphitheater, before arriving at the Grant Grove Visitor Center, where you began.

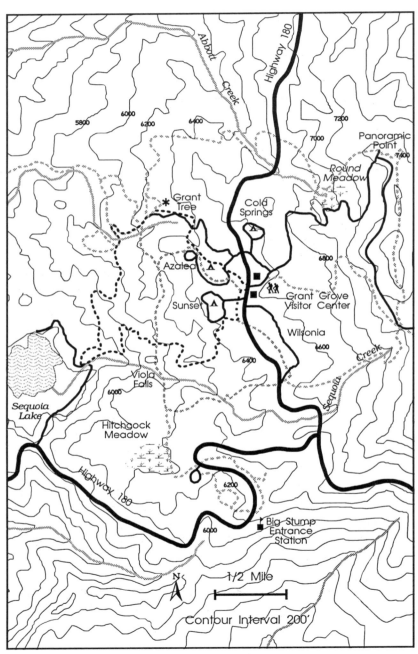

Sunset Trail

SUNSET TRAIL

DISTANCE: 5 Miles

HIKING TIME: 4 Hours

STARTING ELEVATION: 6589'

LOWEST ELEVATION: 5400'

DIFFICULTY: Moderate

USGS MAP: Giant Forest

For those camp tenders who need something exciting to lure them out of their aluminum chairs, this trail offers two beautiful waterfalls, and a lake.

Beginning at the Grant Grove Visitor Center, cross Highway 180 on the painted crosswalk, and head downhill, toward the amphitheater. Follow the trail signs toward Ella Falls, skirting the edge of Sunset Campground.

(If you're staying at Sunset Campground, you can also begin the hike at this point; look for the trail at the entrance to the campground.)

At the southern end of Sunset campground, the trail turns west, again following the sign toward Ella Falls.

The trail descends short switchbacks, passing among some of the most beautiful specimens of sugarpines in all of Kings Canyon. Sugarpines are a five-needle pine with medium-short needles and reddish-brown bark. Look for the long, graceful, but asymmetrical limbs, and the large pine cones.

At about 1 mile you cross an unnamed creek on a wooden footbridge. The small garden of ferns, red willows and azaleas growing beside the creek here would be the envy of any landscape architect.

At about 1 3/4 miles, elevation 6000 feet, you come to the junction of the South Boundary Trail. (A 1/4 mile detour, following the South Boundary Trail to the south, would take you to Viola Falls.) The Sunset Trail continues west.

The trail crosses another unnamed creek, as pretty as the first, and continues to descend, but more steeply now. The bright red triangles you see nailed to the trees are to mark a winter ski trail which follows this route.

2 1/4 miles brings you to Sequoia Creek and Ella Falls, elevation 5600 feet. The waterfall is about 50 feet high, cascading over oddly-eroded granite bowls, amid a lush landscape of azaleas, alders, and willows.

Continuing downhill, at about 2 1/2 miles you reach the park boundary, and arrive at the edge of a private camp owned by the YMCA. As the posted sign informs you, you are welcome to hike here, but you must stay on the trail.

At 2 1/2 miles, elevation 6100 feet, you come to a trail junction. The Sunset Trail continues to the north, uphill.

(By taking a 1/4 mile detour at this point, you can reach Sequoia Lake. At the junction take the downhill trail to the paved road, which is the access road to Sequoia Lake. Cross the road and continue downhill, twice crossing Sequoia Creek on wooden footbridges, before arriving at Sequoia Lake.

In August of 1889, Sequoia Creek was dammed at Mill Flat Meadow. The water from the newly-formed Sequoia Lake was then used to feed a lumber flume which ran 54 miles to Sanger, on the floor of the San Joaquin Valley. The Kings River Lumber Company logged 19,000,000 board feet of timber in this area, and cut down 8,000 giant sequoias. The milled lumber was sent down the flume to Sanger.

At the edge of the pretty, man-made lake there are picnic tables in the shade. Remember, this is private property; do not enter the camp, and return the same way you came.)

From the junction at 6100 feet, the Sunset Trail climbs steeply for just a few hundred feet, where you then meet an old fire road. Actually, before the completion of Highway 180 and the Generals Highway, in 1926, this was the entrance road to the small Grant Grove National Park, established in 1890. The huge Kings Canyon National Park wasn't established until 1940.

In less than 100 yards, you leave the private property and re-enter the park at a gate which marks the boundary. Imagine all the dusty Model A Fords full of carsick tourists who passed this point en route to the General Grant Tree.

You are now on your homeward leg of the Sunset Trail, a slow climb on the gently-graded road, passing through a quiet corner of the park.

At about 4 1/4 miles, elevation 5950 feet, you come to the junction of the Dead Giant Loop, which is described in that chapter. (That short detour provides you with a distant view of Sequoia Lake.)

You now pass a lush meadow, surrounded by medium-size sequoias, and continue on the fire road, uphill.

At about 4 1/2 miles you come to a junction with the North Grove Loop, which is described in that chapter.

You now begin to see some very large sequoias, and at 5 miles, elevation 6350 feet, you arrive at the Grant Tree parking area.

If you don't have a vehicle waiting here, you can hike back to the Grant Grove Visitor Center on the trail which leaves from the east side of this parking area. The distance to the visitor center is 1 mile.

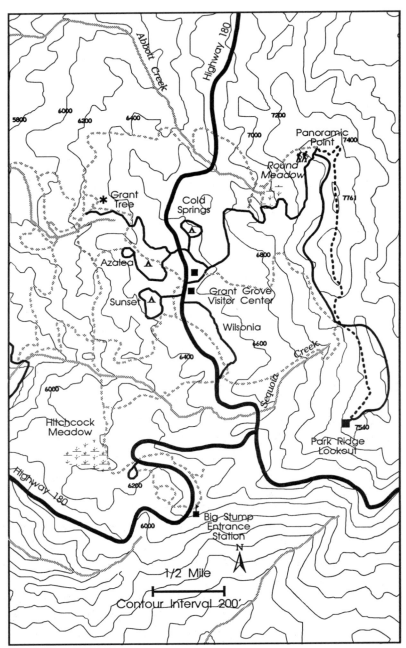

Park Ridge Trail

PARK RIDGE TRAIL

To Panoramic Point and the Fire Lookout

DISTANCE: 2 1/2 Miles to the Fire Lookout
HIKING TIME: 1 1/2 Hours to the Fire Lookout
STARTING ELEVATION: 7360´
HIGHEST ELEVATION: 7761´
DIFFICULTY: Easy to Moderate
USGS MAP: Giant Forest and Tehipite Dome

The expansive vistas along this trail are delightful in the early spring and late fall when the air quality is good. You might be disappointed in the summer, unless you happen to be here following a rain.

This trail is probably best enjoyed in the winter, though in that season you must travel it by skis or snowshoes, beginning at Grant Grove Village. The yellow and red tags you see in the trees along this trail are used to mark the winter ski route.

From the Grant Grove Visitor Center, drive east on the narrow road, past the post office and market. Soon you come to a sign which reads, "Panoramic Point 2.3 miles." The road forks a couple of times, but is well marked. Continue uphill to the Panoramic Point parking area, where there are picnic tables and an outhouse. (Just west of the parking area you see the dirt fire road which leads to the fire lookout; the locked gate blocks vehicle traffic, but you can hike back along that road if you like.)

The trailhead is at the south end of the parking area.

You climb steadily on a paved trail, and in just 200 yards reach Panoramic Point, elevation 7520 feet, where there is a fine view of the backcountry of Kings Canyon. A pair of interpretive signs here helps you identify the distant landmarks.

The trail now follows the ridge top, climbing only gradually, and offering alternating views of the backcountry to the east, and of the foothills and San Joaquin Valley to the west.

The Hume Lake basin, due east of the ridge, was heavily logged in the first decade of this century. Hume Lake itself is a man-made reservoir, originally built to provide water for a flume to carry the rough-cut lumber to the planing mill at Sanger, on the floor of the San Joaquin Valley. In 1919, the National Park Service considered including the Hume Lake area in Sequoia National Park, but when Stephen Mather, the director of the National Park Service, saw the devastation there with his own eyes, he decided against it. After nearly 100 years, the badly-eroded hillsides above the basin have not recovered from the logging damage.

At about 1 mile, you climb the knoll marked 7761 feet on the map. Looking to the south, you may be able to spot the fire lookout, partly hidden in trees.

At about 1 1/2 miles, elevation 7400 feet, you meet the fire road which leads to the lookout. Follow the dirt road south for approximately 50 yards; looking to the right, you now see a wooden sign which marks a trail junction; at this point you leave the road and continue on the trail leading to the south. (Note: The two trails which descend the ridge from this junction are the Manzanita Trail and the Azalea Trail; both trails lead to the Grant Grove Visitor Center.)

Leaving the dense forest of red firs, you enter an area of ponderosa and sugar pines. At about 2 1/4 miles you again meet the fire road, and now follow it to the Park Ridge Fire Lookout, 2 1/2 miles, elevation 7540 feet.

If the lookout is manned (or womanned), it would be courteous of you to shout out your arrival. Remember, this is a residence as well as a work place. If you would like to see the view from the tower, ask for permission before climbing the stairs.

All across the West, fire lookouts have almost become a thing of the past. In Sequoia and Kings Canyon National Parks, only two fire lookouts are still manned: Milk Ranch (off the Mineral King Road), and the one here at Park Ridge. At one time the Park Service used several more fire lookouts (Ash Peaks, Cahoon Rock, Mitchell Peak), but in recent years the Park Service has decided it is cheaper and more efficient to do reconnaissance by airplane during periods of high fire danger. Still, for those park employees lucky enough to get fire lookout duty, it's an enjoyable, though not particularly well-paying, assignment.

You can return to the parking area by the route you came, but most hikers will want to complete the loop by following the fire road. One corner of the fire road passes outside the park, so don't be startled when you come upon a logged area. On your way back, you will have better views of the San Joaquin Valley, and here and there glimpses of the village of Wilsonia, a private community of summer cabins directly below you.

At about 5 miles you again reach the Panoramic Point parking area.

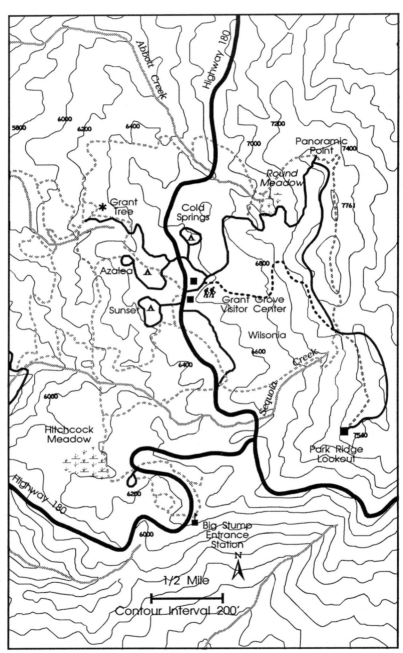

Manzanita Trail

MANZANITA TRAIL

DISTANCE: 1 1/2 Miles

HIKING TIME: 1 Hour

STARTING ELEVATION: 6589ʹ

HIGHEST ELEVATION: 7400ʹ at Park Ridge

DIFFICULTY: Moderate

USGS MAP: Giant Forest

If you've ever driven to the top of Park Ridge, you've probably seen hikers trudging up and down the road, dodging traffic, and muttering angrily to themselves about how all the cars are cluttering up their trail. They need to know about the Manzanita Trail, which would also lead them to the top of Park Ridge, but over a more beautiful route, with better views, and without the danger of becoming a road kill.

Finding the start of this trail is a bit tricky, so read carefully: Begin at the parking area east of the Grant Grove Visitor Center. Follow the paved road northeast, passing below the market. Just north of the market parking area, turn uphill on a smaller paved road, disregarding the sign which reads "Residential Area Only." Continue uphill, past the wood yard. At less than 1/2 mile, just as you can see the large, gray, water-storage tanks ahead, you come to a small wooden sign which marks the head of the Manzanita Trail.

(An alternate way to begin this trail is to walk or drive up the Panoramic Point Road 1.4 miles to Round Meadow, elevation 7000 feet. There's a small turnout there, and the trail is marked by a wooden sign on the south side of the road which reads "Manzanita Trail 0.5." Follow that trail south until you meet the Manzanita Trail.)

The trail begins climbing through a dense forest of white firs and sugarpines. Almost all the work you'll do on this trail is accomplished in the first mile, so go slowly and enjoy the exercise.

At about 1/2 mile, elevation 6880 feet, you meet a short trail which leads from Crystal Springs Campground and the Cedar Springs park service residential area.

At about 3/4 miles, elevation 7120 feet, you meet the short trail which leads from Round Meadow, described in parentheses above.

You now turn in a more southerly direction, and begin to have some excellent 180-degree views of the lower foothills and the San Joaquin Valley to the west. If you look carefully to the southeast, you may be able to spot the Park Ridge Fire Lookout, which is partly hidden by trees.

The trail passes through some dense thickets of manzanita, for which this trail was named. In the late summer, when the manzanita berries are ripe, you might try tasting one of the "little apples," which is what the Spanish name means. They're dry and pulpy—edible, though hardly delectable. If you break apart a pile of bear scat along the trail, you'll find that bears eat manzanita berries by the mouthful, though whether or not they actually digest any is another matter.

The local Indians found the best use for manzanita berries: they ground them into powder, placed the powder in a basket, and poured cool water through it. Early white settlers who tried this manzanita cider said it was the most refreshing drink they'd ever tasted.

During a fire, mature stands of manzanita burn very rapidly, and very hotly. But once the fire has passed, the roots send out vigorous new shoots, which deer and other animals find very nourishing.

As you approach the top of Park Ridge, the manzanita and sugarpines give way to chinquapin and ponderosa pines.

And at 1 1/2 miles, elevation 7400 feet, you meet the dirt fire road which leads to the Park Ridge Fire Lookout. (The road is closed to public vehicles.) Here you have several options:

Turning to the north, you can follow either the fire road or the Park Ridge Trail about 1 1/2 miles to Panoramic Point and parking area. Turning to the south, you can follow either the fire road or the Park Ridge Trail about 1 mile to the Park Ridge Fire Lookout. Or, you can follow the Azalea Trail back to the Grant Grove Visitor Center.

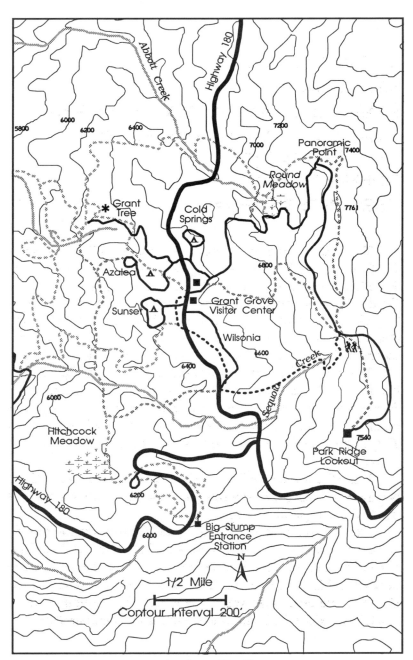

Azalea   Trail

AZALEA TRAIL

DISTANCE: 2 miles

HIKING TIME: 1 Hour

STARTING ELEVATION: 7400´ at Park Ridge

LOWEST ELEVATION: 6589´ at the Grant Grove
Visitor Center

DIFFICULTY: Easy

USGS MAP: Giant Forest

This trail is described here as a route from Park Ridge to the Grant Grove Visitor Center, but of course you can hike it the other way too, if you like. Most hikers take the Manzanita Trail to Park Ridge, then return by way of the Azalea Trail. A lazy alternative would be to have somebody drop you off at the Panoramic Point parking area, hike the Park Ridge Trail, then return to Grant Grove Village by way of the Azalea Trail.

The trailhead can be found on the fire road to the Park Ridge Lookout, 1 1/2 miles from the Panoramic Point parking area. The public isn't allowed to drive on the fire road, but you can reach the trailhead by way of the Manzanita Trail, or the Park Ridge Trail. Look for a wooden trail sign which points the way to Wilsonia.

From the wooden trail sign on the fire road, the Azalea Trail begins descending on fairly steep switchbacks, passing through white firs and ponderosa pines.

At about 1/2 mile you reach a small fork of Sequoia Creek, which may be dry late in the summer. The creek banks are lush with ferns and azaleas. In early summer, when the azaleas are in bloom, this stretch of creek is one of the finest sights in the Grant Grove area. As pretty as they may be, though, azaleas contain a toxin which can cause convulsions and paralysis.

The trail soon crosses the creek on a culvert bridge, and continues descending rapidly, following the course of the creek, and crossing it again.

At about 3/4 miles you begin to see cabins in the village of Wilsonia. This is a private enclave which the government wasn't able to acquire when Grant Grove National Park was established in 1890. Originally, it consisted of 160 acres that were divided into small lots and sold as cabin sites. The Park's long-range goal is to remove all private enclaves within the park boundaries.

The trail now skirts the edge of Wilsonia, and at 1 mile it joins the South Boundary Trail. Here you turn in a more northerly direction, crossing Sequoia Creek for the third time.

The trail immediately crosses a paved road which, if you like, you can follow as it meanders through Wilsonia and back to Highway 180.

The Azalea Trail now follows a route near Highway 180. The trail crosses the highway at Sunset Campground, and passes above the amphitheater, before arriving at the Grant Grove Visitor Center.

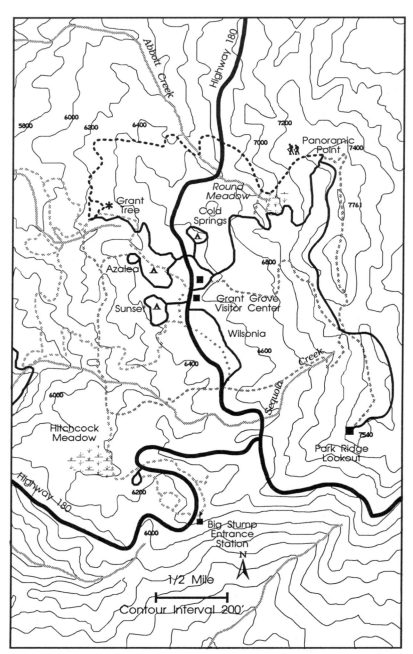

North Boundary Trail

NORTH BOUNDARY TRAIL

DISTANCE: 4 Miles

HIKING TIME: 2 Hours

STARTING ELEVATION: 7360´ at the Panoramic Point Parking Area

LOWEST ELEVATION: 6350´ at the Grant Tree Parking Area

DIFFICULTY: Moderate

USGS MAP: Tehipite Dome and Giant Forest

There are several places where you can begin this trail, depending on whether you're looking for a short hike or a long hike. You can hike it uphill or downhill, depending on whether you are looking for an easy hike, or a challenging one. You can hike it one-way from the Panoramic Point parking area to the Grant Grove parking area, or you can hike it as an 8-mile loop. Read the description below, then select the starting point that is appropriate for you.

The North Boundary Trail is used by the Grant Grove Corrals for taking visitors on horseback rides. For that reason the trail tends to be dusty and well-fertilized. In the summer, save this trail until after a rain heavy enough to settle the dust. In the fall it is ideal.

Please remember that when you meet horses or other stock, the proper trail etiquette is for hikers to step off the trail, on the downhill side, and stand quietly until the horses have passed. This is for your safety, as well as the safety of the animals.

To begin at the Panoramic Point parking area, drive east from the Grant Grove Visitor Center on the narrow road, past the post office and market. Soon you come to a sign which reads, "Panoramic Point 2.3 miles." The road forks a couple of times, but is well marked. Continue uphill to the Panoramic

Point parking area, where there are picnic tables and an outhouse.

There is no sign marking the trailhead. Beginning at the outhouse, walk due west a couple hundred feet until you see a dirt road blocked by a locked gate. (A sign on the gate reads "Do Not Block Access-Fire Lane.") Just 100 feet west of the gate, the trail leaves the dirt road and turns to the southwest, following under the power lines.

The trail now descends steeply, passing through firs, sugarpines, and chinquapin. Through the dense forest you have occasional views to the west.

After about 1 mile, elevation 6950 feet, you reach Round Meadow. Here a short trail leads south to the Park Ridge Road.

The trail now descends through large stands of bitter cherry, chinquapin, and ferns. You can see by the rock walls along this trail that it is quite old. In the early days of the park, these "truck trails," as they were called, were built to provide access, as well as fuel breaks, in the event of a fire. The North Boundary Trail, the Park Ridge Trail, the South Boundary Trail, and the Sunset Trail nearly encircled the original Grant Grove National Park.

At 1 3/4 miles you come to a junction marked by a large wooden trail sign. The short trail to the south leads through Round Meadow, and on to the Park Ridge Road.

The trail continues to descend, a bit less steeply now. And at 2 miles, elevation 6600 feet, you reach Highway 180.

(If you want to start the North Boundary Trail at Highway 180, from the Grant Grove Visitor Center drive north on the highway 1.3 miles. There's a turnout on the east side of the road.)

Cross the highway on the painted crosswalk, and pick up the trail again on the west side.

The trail descends moderately, and soon crosses Abbott Creek on a wooden footbridge. The trail now follows above the creek, which is lined with ferns and red willow.

As the trail approaches the park boundary, you have some good views to the north. Notice that on the Sequoia National Forest side of the boundary there has been some logging. Here, where the forest is highly-visible to the public, the Forest Service has chosen to select cut, rather than clearcut; that is, only mature trees have been taken, leaving a healthy, varied, and well-groomed forest. Logging companies prefer to clearcut, however, arguing that it is too expensive to select cut.

At about 3 miles, elevation 6450 feet, you arrive at a junction. The trail turning uphill, to the southeast, leads to the corrals. The North Boundary Trail continues downhill.

You now pass through areas where the Park Service has been conducting prescribed burns to reduce the accumulation of forest debris, and to thin the dense stands of white firs. This also produces a healthy, varied, well-groomed forest, but by natural means.

The trail now begins to descend more steeply, as the white firs give way to sugarpines and cedars, with a scattering of dogwoods.

Circling back to the east, the trail begins climbing, and you soon see the first giant sequoias on the perimeter of Grant Grove.

At about 4 miles, you meet the General Grant Tree Loop, just above the Gamlin Cabin. A sign there directs you to the parking area.

If you left your car at the Panoramic Point parking area, and want to return there by trail, you can retrace the North Boundary Trail, or you can use the following description: At the east end of the General Grant Tree parking area is a trail that leads to the Grant Grove Visitor Center; from there you take the Manzanita Trail east to Park Ridge, and follow the Park Ridge Trail north to the Panoramic Point parking area. Total mileage from the Grant Tree parking area to the Panoramic Point parking area is about 4 miles.

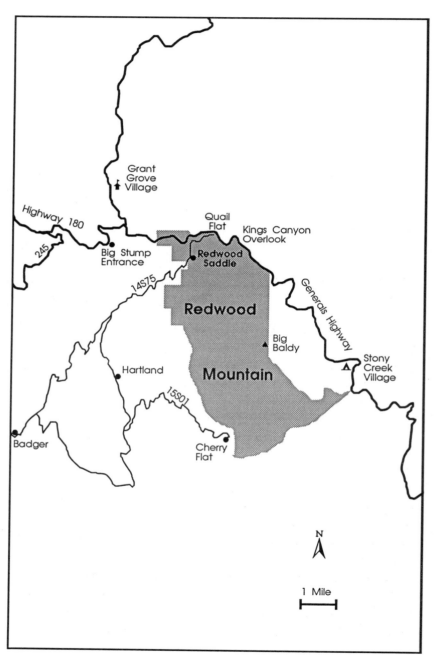

Redwood Mountain

INTRODUCTION

TO

REDWOOD MOUNTAIN

Although thousands of visitors to Kings Canyon National Park drive within a stone's throw of Redwood Mountain every year, not many visitors ever find their way on to its trails. Yet for day hikers, particularly those who love hiking through quiet groves of sequoias, Redwood Mountain is as fine as anything Kings Canyon has to offer.

The Redwood Mountain Grove is the largest existing grove of sequoias in the world. (The Converse Basin Grove, remember, was the world's largest before it was clearcut in the 1880s.) Though there has been some light logging on Redwood Mountain, most of it before the turn of the century, there are still more than 2100 giant sequoias there larger than 10 feet in diameter. There are also some very fine sugarpines scattered among the sequoias, and along Redwood Creek is one of the finest displays of dogwoods in the park.

When the tiny Grant Grove National Park was established in 1890, Redwood Mountain was in private hands, and small-scale loggers were still cutting down giant sequoias, mostly for fence posts and shake shingles. Even after the establishment of Kings Canyon National Park, on March 4, 1940, the Redwood Mountain area remained in private hands. But soon after, the government was able to buy the land, and on June 21, 1940, with a proclamation by President Franklin Roosevelt, Redwood Mountain was added to Kings Canyon National Park.

During the 1960s and '70s it was feared that the sequoias on Redwood Mountain weren't reproducing in adequate numbers to assure the survival of the grove. The single greatest reason for this decline in reproduction was believed to be man's suppression of fire. Giant sequoias are dependent upon fire to clear a bed in the forest soil where their seeds can germinate. In the early 70s, the Park Service began a series of prescribed burns on Redwood Mountain, and today young sequoia seedlings can be found growing there by the thousands.

Three of the trails in this section begin at Redwood Saddle. The description to Redwood Saddle is given here so it won't have to be repeated for each trail: If you are coming from the north on the Generals Highway, drive 5.4 miles from the Grant Grove Visitor Center. If you are coming from the south on the Generals Highway, drive 8.1 miles from Stony Creek. The turnoff to Redwood Saddle is on the south side of the highway, and is marked by a small brown sign which reads "Redwood Saddle Road." (Directly across the highway is the Hume Lake turnoff, marked by a large metal sign.)

The road to Redwood Saddle is unpaved but graded, and is generally suitable for passenger vehicles. Drive down the road 1.8 miles. At the saddle you will see, on your right, the large cabin which at one time was used as the park superintendent's summer home. Here you turn left and, after passing through a break in a large downed sequoia, arrive at the parking area.

While hiking on Redwood Mountain, you will find both the newer metal trail signs, as well as some very old wooden signs. There are many discrepancies among the distances quoted on the signs, but don't let that worry you. This guidebook tries to reconcile some of those discrepancies and arrive at the most realistic estimates for distances on the mountain.

Notice, too, that the Redwood Canyon Trail is referred to on some trail signs as the Redwood Creek Trail. They are the same trail.

Be sure to carry water while hiking on Redwood Mountain. You may find water in the creeks in spring and early summer, but in most years they have dried out by midsummer.

And finally, to close this introduction to Redwood Mountain, we have a few phrases of purple prose from John Muir: "Here the sequoias attained full possession of the forest for several miles, covering the hill...in magnificent order. The sky outline... I shall never forget—such swelling domes of verdure so effortlessly poised in the cool blue sky."

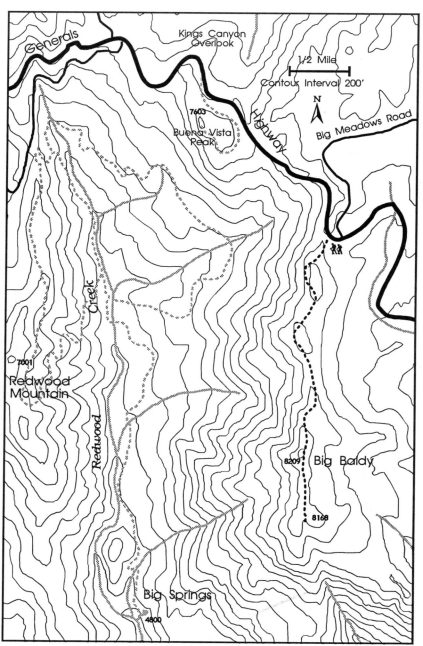

Generals

Kings Canyon
Overlook

1/2 Mile

Contour Interval 200'

N

7603

Buena Vista
Peak

Highway

Big Meadows Road

Creek

7001

Redwood
Mountain

Redwood

8209   Big Baldy

8168

Big Springs

4800

Big Baldy Trail

BIG BALDY TRAIL

DISTANCE: 2 3/4 Miles
HIKING TIME: 1 1/2 Hours
STARTING ELEVATION: 7600′
HIGHEST ELEVATION: 8209′
DIFFICULTY: Easy
USGS MAP: Giant Forest

Save this trail for a clear spring or fall day. If you hike it in the summer, you will likely be disappointed by the smog to the west. But when the sky is clear, the Big Baldy Trail has one of the finest views of any day hike in the park.

The Big Baldy trailhead is on the Generals Highway, about 6.8 miles south of the Grant Grove Visitor Center, and about 4.9 miles north of Stony Creek Village. On the south side of the highway, look for the wooden sign which reads "Big Baldy Trailhead." The parking area is small, and it's located on a blind curve; use caution here when turning in from the highway.

The trail follows the ridge of Big Baldy, crossing back and forth between Kings Canyon National Park (to the west), and Sequoia National Forest (to the east). Dogs, guns and bicycles are not allowed.

This trail makes an excellent cross-country ski trail in the winter. When the trail is covered by snow, follow the bright red metal tags nailed about 10 feet high in the trees.

After climbing briefly through a dense forest of red firs, you soon have good views of Redwood Mountain to the west, and of the foothills beyond.

At about 1/2 mile you gain a view of the east, particularly of the rocky Silliman Crest.

You now pass through several patches of currant bushes. In the late summer these bright red berries are edible, if not exactly tasty to the human palate. Still, they're an important source of food for wildlife.

You also see chinquapin, a shrub with leaves dark green on the top and yellow on the underside. In the late summer, when the chinquapin's catkins are developed, the plant has a sharply pungent odor.

At about 1 mile you have a good view of Big Baldy itself, almost due south.

Looking to the southwest you see a long foothill valley. That is Eshom Valley, whose Indian name, Cha-ha-du, means "a place where clover grows the year around."

In the fall of 1872, Eshom Valley became the site of one the last big Indian ghost dances. Ghost dances began when a Paiute medicine man, named Tavibo, prophesied that dead Indians would be resurrected, and white settlers would be destroyed, if the people would perform the dances he prescribed. The ghost dance ritual spread like fever to desperate Indian tribes all across the continent. The ghost dance held at Eshom Valley attracted perhaps five hundred people, and lasted for six days.

At about 2 1/4 miles, elevation 8209 feet, you reach the summit of Big Baldy. Because of the way Big Baldy extends out from the crest of the Kaweahs, its panoramic view is exceptional. Looking to the south, you can see as far as Mineral King. To the east, you can see the Great Western Divide. To the northeast, you can see peaks on the main crest of the Sierra Nevada.

Keep in mind that there is the possibility of lightning on Big Baldy. If the sky is cloudy you should descend to a lower elevation.

The trail continues for another 1/2 mile, to the knoll marked 8168 feet on the map, where you have a view of the distinctive rock formation to the southeast known as Chimney Rock, and of the lower Redwood Canyon.

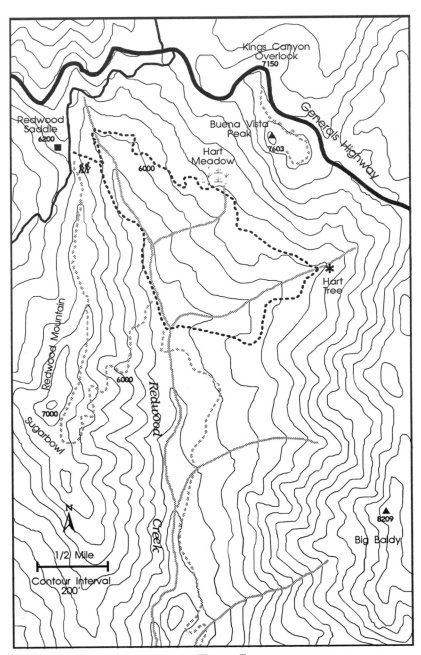

Hart Tree Loop

HART TREE LOOP

DISTANCE: 6 3/4 Miles
HIKING TIME: 5 Hours
STARTING ELEVATION: 6200´
HIGHEST ELEVATION: 6400´ at Hart Meadow
DIFFICULTY: Strenuous
USGS MAP: Giant Forest

This trail is probably the most beautiful and scenic at Redwood Mountain, and the historical sites along its route are interesting as well. The distance may be a bit long for some hikers, but the elevation gain is not great, and most hikers will find this makes an excellent all-day hike.

The Hart Tree Loop begins at the Redwood Saddle parking area, which is described in the introduction to this section.

At the east end of the Redwood Saddle parking area, look for the trailhead sign for the Redwood Canyon Trail. The Hart Tree Loop follows that trail for the first 1/2 mile.

The trail begins by quickly descending 200 feet to the canyon bottom, passing through a group of large sequoias. If you look carefully, you can see patches of wild strawberries growing here.

At about 1/2 mile you come to a trail sign which reads "Hart Tree Trail." Here you leave the Redwood Canyon Trail, and turn to the northeast.

You cross the head of Redwood Creek, elevation 6000 feet, and soon come to an old logging camp known as Barton's Post Camp.

The logging on Redwood Mountain was neither as aggressive, nor as destructive, as that at Converse Basin and Hume Lake. These were small-scale operations, mostly run by farmers from the San Joaquin Valley looking for a productive way to spend their summers out of the heat of the Valley.

At Barton's Post Camp you see the stump of a large sequoia with notches 4 to 6 inches wide carved into it about 10 feet above the ground. These notches were used to support a wooden scaffolding, which allowed the loggers to work above the tree's butt swell.

You also see at this camp that several of the felled sequoias were left unused. This is because redwood is very brittle, and the trees tend to shatter when they hit the ground. The loggers often spent a considerable amount of time digging a bed, then lining it with trees branches to cushion the fall. But if the tree feller wasn't perfectly accurate in reckoning where the tree would land, the time, and the tree, were wasted.

At about 3/4 miles you cross a small creek, and come to an old fire-hollowed sequoia that was converted into a summer residence, known as Redwood Log Cabin. This practical method of acquiring a rain-tight shelter was used by loggers, ranchers, and settlers throughout the southern Sierra. Notice how shake shingles were used to close off gaps in the shelter, and that a rock and mortar fireplace was added at one end.

You now begin climbing fairly steeply—the hardest work you will do on this loop. At about 1 1/2 miles you come to a rocky knoll, which makes a good place to stop and rest for a few minutes. Here you have good views of Redwood Mountain, as well as Big Baldy to the southeast, and Buena Vista Peak to the northeast. Both peaks have trails to their summits, and those trails are described in this section.

The trail now turns in a more northerly direction, and at about 1 3/4 miles you reach Hart Meadow, elevation 6400 feet. This small meadow, on the uphill side of the trail, was named for William Hart, a cattleman from Eshom Valley. On the edges of Hart Meadow, you see several brilliant-green stalks of skunk cabbage, also known as false hellebore. Those hikers who have forgotten to carry toilet paper may want to familiarize themselves with the large, soft leaves of this plant.

Just beyond Hart Meadow, you reach the fringes of the Buena Vista Grove, which contains some of the largest and most beautiful giant sequoias in the park. Take your time to enjoy this quiet and secluded grove.

At 2 miles you come to Tunnel Log, where the trail passes through a hollow sequoia.

You now descend gradually to the East Fork of Redwood Creek, in a fairly deep gully. Just a few hundred feet beyond the creek, and at a total distance of 3 miles, you come to a sign which reads "Hart Tree   100 Yards," and points uphill.

The Hart Tree has a peculiar and interesting base; a large arch extends from one side as a kind of architectural support. All large sequoia's grow buttresses around their base, but a ground fire has fashioned this one into a kind of flying buttress.

You now descend to a small, unnamed creek which features a short waterfall in the spring.

At 4 1/4 miles, you come to the Fallen Goliath , a very large fire-hollowed sequoia on the uphill side of the trail. Some of the graffiti carved into this log is very old.

4 3/4 miles brings you to the bottom of the canyon, and Redwood Creek, elevation 5500 feet. This is a beautiful place, lush with dogwoods, alders, and ferns, and it makes a very good spot to rest or have lunch. Here you cross over to the west side of the creek, where you again pick up the trail.

You now turn north on the homeward leg of this loop, following Redwood Creek, and climbing only moderately. At about 5 miles you come to the junction of the Sugarbowl Trail, which follows the ridge of Redwood Mountain.

Continuing up canyon, at about 5 1/2 miles, the trail begins climbing more steeply, as it rises above the canyon floor. This section of trail is particularly beautiful in June, when the dogwoods are in bloom.

And at about 6 1/4 miles you return to the junction where you began the Hart Tree Loop. Turn west, uphill, and complete the short 1/2 mile back to the parking area.

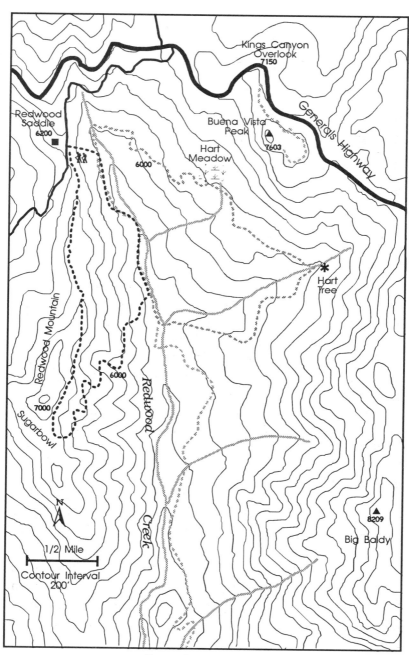

Sugarbowl Trail

SUGARBOWL TRAIL

DISTANCE: 6 3/4 Miles (a loop hike)
HIKING TIME: 4 Hours
STARTING ELEVATION: 6200ʹ
HIGHEST ELEVATION: 6750ʹ
DIFFICULTY: Moderate
USGS MAP: Giant Forest

This is probably the easiest hike in the Redwood Mountain area, and gives hikers a chance to see both the top of Redwood Mountain, as well as Redwood Creek, at the bottom.

The trailhead for the Sugarbowl Trail is at Redwood Saddle parking area. Directions to Redwood Saddle are given in the introduction to this section. Look for the trailhead at the south end of the Redwood Saddle parking area.

The trail follows the ridge of Redwood Mountain, climbing steeply at first, but soon leveling off to a gentle grade, passing through groups of large sequoias, sugarpines, and firs.

This area of Redwood Mountain was burned under controlled conditions by the Park Service in the early 1970s. You can see that some of the trees have recent burn scars, but also notice how open the forest floor is, and how relatively free it is of dead trees and other forest litter. Before the prescribed burns in this area, the forest was so cluttered with dead debris that almost no new seedlings had a chance to grow. Now there is a healthy mixture of young and old trees, as well as a healthy variety of trees.

You pass some old sequoia stumps that date back to the late 1800s, long before this area was included in Kings Canyon National Park. Fortunately, Redwood Mountain was never logged as heavily as the Big Stump, Converse Basin, and Hume Lake areas.

In the soft dirt along this trail there are many ant lion cones, about the diameter of a quarter, and an inch deep. Catch an ant, carefully drop it into one of the cones, then watch what happens. The ant lion, which lives just beneath the surface at the bottom of the cone, immediately captures the ant and drags it underground. To capture the ant lion, drop another ant into a cone, but this time use a slip of paper to scoop the lion out as soon as he pounces on the ant.

After about 1 mile, looking to the west, you have occasional glimpses of the foothills, and of the San Joaquin Valley beyond. To the northeast you have views of Buena Vista Peak, and to the southeast, views of Big Baldy. Both of those peaks are accessible by trails described in this section.

After about 1 1/4 miles, the forest begins to thin somewhat, as the trail enters an area of scattered black oaks and ponderosa pines.

At about 2 miles, this trail reaches its highest point, 6750 feet. The trail now begins descending into a group of large sequoias. Known as the Sugarbowl, this area was once said to contain the largest number of board feet of growing timber in one acre in the world.

At 2 1/2 miles you come to a very old wooden sign nailed to a fir tree about 24 inches in diameter; the sign gives the mileage to various points at Redwood Mountain. (Note that at this point the shortest and easiest route back to the parking area is the way you came.)

The trail now makes a turn to the east, and begins a long, winding descent into Redwood Canyon, passing through large patches of manzanita and bear clover. This is a quiet and remote corner of Redwood Mountain, the kind of place favored by black bears; look for their tracks in the soft dirt. It's also low enough, and warm enough for rattlesnakes. Be sure to watch your footing as you pass through the bear clover.

As you approach the bottom of the canyon, you begin to see some very dense thickets of young sequoias that have sprouted here since the last fire. Without fire to prepare the seedbed, sequoia seeds rarely germinate.

At the bottom of the canyon, at an elevation of 5500 feet, and a total of 5 miles, you come to the junction of the Redwood Canyon Trail, marked by a metal sign. There are pretty places here along Redwood Creek to rest or have lunch.

You now turn north on the homeward leg of this loop, following Redwood Creek, and climbing only moderately.

At about 5 1/2 miles the trail begins climbing more steeply, as it rises above the canyon floor. This section of trail is particularly beautiful in June, when the dogwoods are in bloom.

And at about 6 1/4 miles you come to the junction of the Hart Tree Loop. Turn west, uphill, and complete the short 1/2 mile back to the parking area.

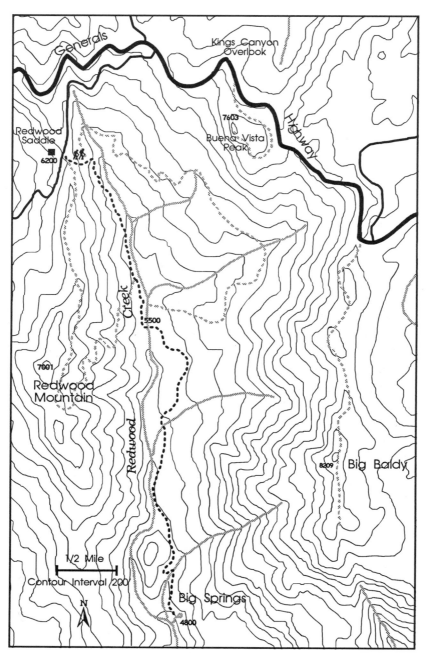

Redwood Canyon Trail

REDWOOD CANYON TRAIL

DISTANCE: 2 1/4 Miles to Redwood Creek
Crossing; 6 1/2 Miles to Big Springs
HIKING TIME: 1 1/2 Hours to Redwood Creek
Crossing; 3 Hours to Big Springs
STARTING ELEVATION: 6200´
LOWEST ELEVATION: 4800´ at Big Springs
DIFFICULTY: Moderate to Strenuous
USGS MAP: Giant Forest

The first 2 miles of this trail are among the most beautiful at Redwood Mountain, and the sequoias are among the most beautiful in all of Sequoia and Kings Canyon National Parks. Those hikers who are looking for the best of Redwood Mountain, with the least amount of work, should consider hiking this trail only as far as the Redwood Creek crossing. Those hikers looking for a more challenging day should consider hiking all the way to Big Springs.

Note that trail signs refer to this as both the Redwood Canyon Trail and the Redwood Creek Trail. They are the same trail, so don't be confused.

The Redwood Canyon Trail begins at the Redwood Saddle parking area, which is described in the introduction to this section. Look for the trailhead sign at the east side of the Redwood Saddle parking area.

The trail begins by quickly descending 200 feet to the canyon bottom, passing through a group of large sequoias. As you can see, this trail was once a road. Originally, it was used by loggers in the late 1800s, later by tungsten miners during World War II, and finally as a fire access road. It has been closed to all vehicle traffic since the late 1970s, and it is slowly narrowing back a trail.

At about 1/2 mile you come to the junction of the Hart Tree Loop. The Redwood Canyon Trail continues to your right, south.

The trail now approaches Redwood Creek, and gradually descends to the lower canyon, passing through groves of large sequoias, alders, and dogwoods. This section of trail is very beautiful in all seasons, but it is exceptionally beautiful in June, when the creek is flowing and the dogwoods are in bloom.

At 1 3/4 miles you come to the junction of the Sugarbowl Trail. Continue down canyon, and at 2 miles, elevation 5500 feet, you again come to a junction with the Hart Tree Loop. This is a very pretty spot to rest or have lunch. For those hikers looking for an easy day, this makes a good turnaround point.

Continue down canyon, and at 2 1/4 miles the trail crosses to the east side of Redwood Creek.

The trail now climbs gradually, leaving the creek for a while, as it contours around the lower side of Big Baldy Ridge.

At about 3 3/4 miles you cross an unnamed creek, thick with alders, but dry in late summer.

The trail draws within sight of Redwood Creek again, though in a typical year Redwood Creek is often dry at this elevation.

The forest is now dominated by dense thickets of cedars and white firs. Thimbleberries are also abundant here; they're related to the raspberry, and the berries themselves are quite similar, though the leaves of the thimbleberry look more like grape leaves. Thimbleberries are sweet and delicious, and if you happen to be here when they're ripe you should stop and gather a handful.

At about 4 miles, if you look carefully on the east side of the trail, you can see an entrance to the Lilburn Cave. The cave entrance is about 15 feet off the trail, in a marble formation, and with a medium-size cedar growing directly above it. Lilburn Cave is the longest cave in California; it is known to be at least 6 1/2 miles long, and could be much longer. The entrance is just big enough for a person to enter, but unless you are an experienced spelunker, with the proper safety equipment, you should not attempt to enter this cave.

At 5 miles, elevation 5200 feet, you come to the Redwood Cabin, which was originally built and occupied by a tungsten miner named Lilburn. During World War II, tungsten, which is used for hardening steel, was in great demand, and small-scale mines such as this one appeared all over the southern Sierra. The cabin has been rebuilt, and is now used by research groups. There is also a picnic table here, as well as good places to rest.

Beyond Redwood Cabin the trail is not regularly maintained. Though it is passable, this route should only be attempted by experienced hikers.

The trail descends into, and then crosses, a side canyon. Several trees have fallen across the trail, and in some places you must watch carefully to follow the route.

You pass through a grove of black oaks 50 feet tall, and come to a point where there is a partial view of lower Redwood Canyon. The trail now descends sharply.

At about 6 1/2 miles, elevation 4800 feet, the trail appears to deadend at Redwood Creek. But looking down canyon, about 300 feet away, you can see a lone, medium-size sequoia growing on the east bank of the creek. Carefully pick your way down the creek bottom to that sequoia, which acts as a kind of guardian of Big Springs.

The spring itself gushes from the mountainside almost as a full-size creek, and the water is cold enough to give you a headache if you drink it. Where the water from the spring flows into Redwood Creek there is a fine, white sandy beach. Notice there are trout here over 6 inches long, which means that Big Springs flows consistently enough, even in drought years, to sustain a permanent fish population.

Big Springs represents one of the great mysteries of the southern Sierra. In the springtime, Big Springs, which is technically known as an "ebb and flow spring," will sometimes run in heads, like a geyser. The spring rises from Lilburn Cave, which periodically flushes with water—that is, it quickly fills with water, then the water recedes. There are only a few caves in the world where this phenomenon has been observed, and there is no proven explanation for it; one theory involves a siphoning effect; another theory relies on mud and sands which periodically become saturated with water.

At one time, the trail continued down canyon to Cherry Flat, but that trail hasn't been maintained in many years, and the route is now impassable.

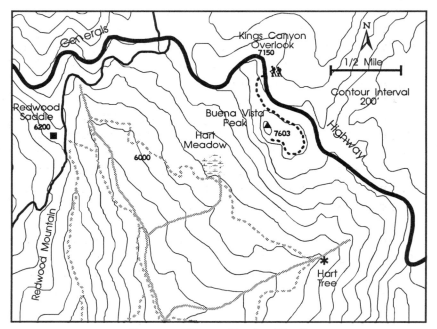

Buena Vista Peak Trail

BUENA VISTA PEAK TRAIL

DISTANCE: 1 Mile

HIKING TIME: 45 Minutes

STARTING ELEVATION: 7150'

HIGHEST ELEVATION: 7603'

DIFFICULTY: Easy

USGS MAP: Giant Forest

This trail is a bit too close to the Generals Highway to offer the peace and quiet most day hikers are looking for. But it makes a good warm-up hike, and the view from the top is at least twice as good as the view from the nearby Kings Canyon Overlook.

The parking area for this trail is just south of the Kings Canyon Overlook, on the west side of the Generals Highway, about 6.7 miles south of Grant Grove Visitor Center, or about 6.8 miles north of Stony Creek Village. A large metal sign marks the parking area. You can also park at the Kings Canyon Overlook parking area, and walk south on the highway 0.1 miles to the Buena Vista Peak trailhead.

Note that this trail is not shown on the USGS map.

The trail begins by gradually contouring up the side of Buena Vista Peak, passing through mixed conifers and manzanita, as well as some oddly-eroded granite boulders. After less than 1/4 mile, looking to the south, you have a view of your destination, the rocky dome of exfoliated granite. Looking to the northeast, you have a good view of Buck Rock, and you can even faintly see the fire lookout tower on the top.

The trail continues contouring around to the south side of Buena Vista Peak, then follows the ridge to the top.

"Buena Vista" in Spanish means "beautiful view," and the name is well deserved here.

Near the summit of Buena Vista Peak there are several ponderosa pines with deformed tops, most of them the victims of lightning. When a tree is struck by lightning, the moisture in the wood is vaporized so quickly that the tree literally explodes. Often, the lower portion of the tree survives, and several of the lower limbs turn skyward, trying to replace the lost top.

Keep in mind while you are on Buena Vista Peak that there is a danger of lightning here. If there are clouds in the sky, or if you can feel electricity in the air, descend to a lower elevation.

Looking immediately to the west, you can see Redwood Mountain, and the Sierra foothills beyond that; the meadow directly below the summit is Hart Meadow. To the south you see Big Baldy. To the east you see the peaks of the Great Western Divide, and more to the northeast you see peaks on the main crest of the Sierra Nevada.

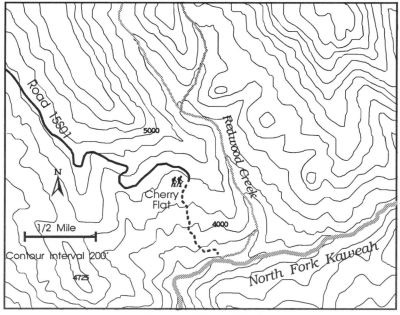

Cherry Flat Trail

CHERRY FLAT TRAIL

DISTANCE: 3/4 Miles
HIKING TIME: 45 Minutes
STARTING ELEVATION: 4300´ at Cherry Flat
LOWEST ELEVATION: 3600´
DIFFICULTY: Moderate
USGS MAP: Giant Forest

Several years ago it was possible to hike from Big Springs, in lower Redwood Canyon, to Cherry Flat. That trail is no longer maintained, and the route is so brushy that trying to follow the old route is not practical. But it is possible to reach the confluence of Redwood Creek with the North Fork of the Kaweah by way of the Cherry Flat Trail.

This is one of the least-used trails in this guide, mostly because the trailhead is so far out of the way. The trail is short, and the drive to the trailhead is long, but both road and trail are interesting, and offer a look at a corner of the Kings Canyon country most people never see.

Also, this trail is at its best in the spring or fall, though the road conditions during those times may be at their worst.

To find this trailhead you will need the current map of Sequoia National Forest. Beginning from either Highway 180 (from Fresno), or Highway 198 (from Visalia), take county road 245 to Badger. Turn east on county road 469 (also known as the Whitaker Forest Road), and drive to Eshom Valley Drive, which is still road 469. Pass through Eshom Valley, and Tarbell Pocket, to Pierce Valley Drive (county road 466). Turn east, uphill, and drive 1.5 miles to forest service road 15S01, marked by a brown fiberglass post. This is a dirt road, generally suitable for two-wheel-drive vehicles, though there may be times when four-wheel drive is necessary. Drive 6 miles to the end of road 15S01.

Be sure to park so you aren't blocking the small turnaround area.

Look for the trail at the south end of the parking area. There is no sign marking the trailhead, but the trail is broad and easy to see.

Note that the trail shown on the USGS map is no longer in existence. The map in this guide shows the current trail.

The trail descends steeply through ponderosa pines, black oaks, live oaks, laurel, and some very tall stands of manzanita. There's a tremendous variety of plant life here in the transition between the foothill belt and the yellow-pine belt.

Looking back to the north you have a striking view of Big Baldy, which overlooks the heart of Redwood Canyon. Looking to the south, across the North Fork of the Kaweah and into Sequoia National Park, you may see a trace of the old road climbing Pine Ridge to Hidden Springs.

By 1/4 mile you leave the pines, and enter dense thickets of chamise, buck brush, and manzanita.

At about 1/2 mile the trail turns more to the east. You can now hear the North Fork of the Kaweah, and even see it occasionally through the brush. You have now entered Kings Canyon National Park, though there is no sign marking the boundary.

And at about 3/4 miles, elevation 3600 feet, you reach the confluence of Redwood Creek and the North Fork of the Kaweah. Here the river has eroded beautifully-sculpted bowls into the granite. Just above the confluence you find a flat area under the shade of live oaks where you can rest.

The river canyon is extremely steep and rugged at this point, and you should use great caution, particularly in the spring and early summer when the water level is high.

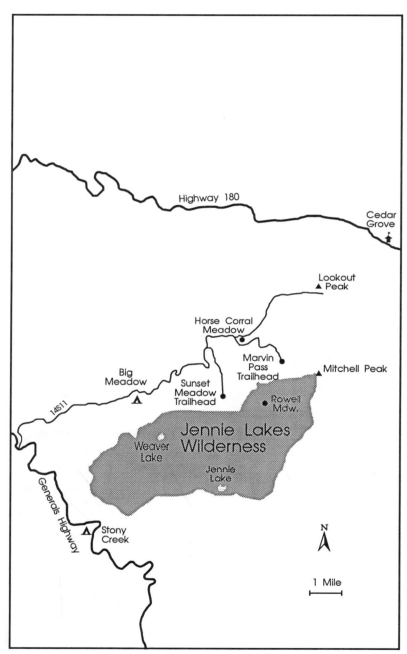

Jennie Lakes Wilderness

INTRODUCTION
TO
JENNIE LAKES WILDERNESS

Although the visitor use in the Jennie Lakes Wilderness increased somewhat after it was designated a wilderness in 1984, there are still times here in the spring and fall when you can hike all day long without seeing another soul.

At 10,500 acres, the Jennie Lakes Wilderness is small enough that any point within its boundaries is within reach of the day hiker. And for a small wilderness, it has a surprising degree of variety, from the summit of Mitchell Peak at 10,365 feet, to Jennie and Weaver lakes, to Rowell Meadow, and to the rugged Boulder Creek canyon. It's a beautiful wilderness, and with the exception of a few overgrazed areas, it is still well preserved.

Although cattle grazing is considered by many to be in conflict with wildlife management, and with the preservation of native plants, the current wilderness legislation allows grazing in the Jennie Lakes Wilderness. Even in the Sugarloaf and Williams Meadow area of Kings Canyon National Park, some grazing is still allowed on leases that existed before the establishment of the park.

In the early days of this area, Daniel P. Zumwalt, a Tulare County attorney, and land agent for the much-hated Southern Pacific Railroad, bought many of the valuable meadow lands near Horse Corral Meadow for as little as $2.50 per acre. His foster son, Walter Goins, together with a partner named Jesse Agnew, drove cattle in this area for many years. Every summer the cattle herds were driven from Orosi (in the San Joaquin Valley), over Redwood Saddle, into the Kings Canyon country.

Agnew later became infamous for killing the last grizzly bear in California, at Horse Corral Meadow in 1922. He said the bear had been molesting his cattle.

Sam Ellis, an early rancher and settler in Tulare County, has left his stamp all over the Jennie Lakes Wilderness. He named Jennie Lake after his wife, and Marvin Pass after his son. Elsewhere in the area there's an Ellis Meadow and an Ellis Creek.

A word of caution: Most of the trailheads in the Jennie Lake Wilderness are reached by the Big Meadow Road. It is narrow and dangerous, though generally well-maintained, and well-marked. The road is partly paved, but mostly dirt. To avoid accidents, keep your speed down, and stay on your own side of the road.

A map showing the roads of Sequoia National Forest can be bought at the National Park Service visitor centers at Ash Mountain, Lodgepole, Grant Grove, and Cedar Grove. It is strongly recommended that you buy that map before trying to find your way anywhere in the Sequoia National Forest. Because of logging operations on forest service lands, the roads are changing almost constantly, and not even the most recent maps show all the current roads.

Note, particularly, that many of the trails in the Jennie Lakes Wilderness have been re-routed since the last printing of the USGS maps for this area. Also, the old cabin shown on the USGS maps at Rowell Meadow Creek has been replaced by a newer cabin 1/4 mile to the west. The maps in this guidebook have been drawn to show the current trail locations, as well as the location of the new cabin.

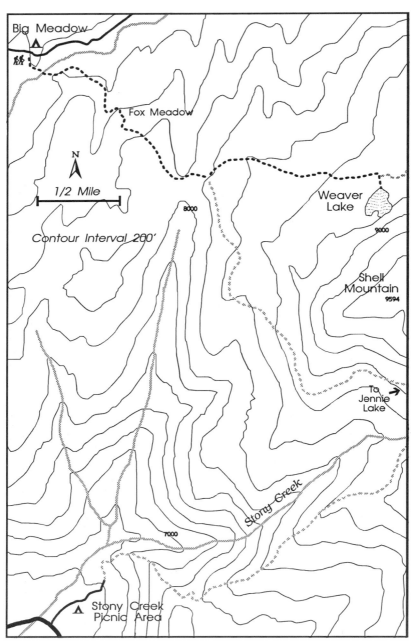

Weaver Lake Trail

WEAVER LAKE TRAIL

DISTANCE: 3 1/2 Miles

HIKING TIME: 2 1/2 Hours

STARTING ELEVATION: 7600´

HIGHEST ELEVATION: 8720´

DIFFICULTY: Moderate

USGS MAP: Giant Forest

The Sierra Nevada is famous for its beautiful alpine lakes. But there aren't many natural lakes in the southern Sierra that can be reached in just a couple hours of walking. Weaver Lake is the exception; moreover, it's that most unusual of alpine lakes—one warm enough to swim in. For lake lovers, Weaver Lake has to be the best deal in the Kings Canyon country.

The Weaver Lake Trail begins at Big Meadow campground. On the Generals Highway, drive south 6.9 miles from the Grant Grove Visitor Center, or north 4.8 miles from Stony Creek. This brings you to the Big Meadow turnoff (forest service road 14S11), which is marked with a large metal sign that reads "Big Meadow." Turn east and drive 3.8 miles to Big Meadow campground. There's a small parking area on the south side of the road, directly across from the guard station.

The trailhead is marked by a brown fiberglass post. As you begin hiking south, watch closely because the trail is difficult to follow as it passes through the campground.

At the south end of the campground, the trail crosses Big Meadow Creek, then turns more to the east, climbing through lodgepole pines, red firs, and Jeffrey pines.

At about 3/4 miles, you cross a small creek lush with ferns. You now begin having some good views of the Monarch Divide, to the distant north.

At 1 1/2 miles, and an elevation of about 8000 feet, after passing through an area that has been heavily logged, you come to Fox Meadow, where there is a small wooden sign and a trail register.

2 miles, and an elevation of 8200 feet, brings you to a trail junction. The trail to Jennie Lake turns to the south; the trail to Weaver Lake continues to the east.

Just past the trail sign, you come to a small creek where you find a good place to rest. The creek drains from Poison Meadow, named by early cattle ranchers because of the poisonous feed—possibly lupine or larkspur—which was growing there.

At about 2 1/4 miles, you come to a wooden sign which marks the boundary of the Jennie Lakes Wilderness. The trail continues climbing gradually through a forest of red firs.

At about 3 miles the trail approaches the edge of a long stringer meadow which follows the outlet of Weaver Lake. Looking to the south you can see Shell Mountain, which is the granite backdrop of Weaver Lake.

You cross the stringer meadow, and another 1/2 mile brings you to Weaver Lake, a pretty, medium-size lake, with small campsites along its shore.

A footpath circles the lake. Fish are abundant, but very small. Look for western blueberries growing on shrubs 1 foot to 2 feet tall; when they're ripe, in midsummer, they're sweet and delicious.

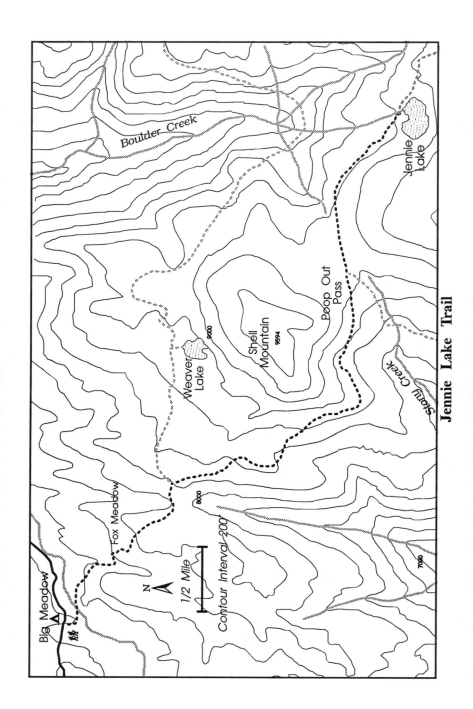

Jennie Lake Trail

JENNIE LAKE TRAIL

From Big Meadow

DISTANCE: 7 Miles
HIKING TIME: 4 Hours
STARTING ELEVATION: 7600´
HIGHEST ELEVATION: 9150´ at Poop Out Pass
DIFFICULTY: Strenuous
USGS MAP: Giant Forest

This trail covers the breadth of Jennie Lakes Wilderness, and then some, before reaching the wilderness area's namesake, Jennie Lake. The trail isn't so strenuous as to put it beyond the reach of day hikers, though. Active fishermen often hike to the lake and back in a day. For ambitious hikers, this trail even continues on to JO Pass.

The Jennie Lake Trail begins at the Big Meadow campground. On the Generals Highway, drive south 6.9 miles from the Grant Grove Visitor Center, or north 4.8 miles from Stony Creek. This brings you to the Big Meadow turnoff (forest service road 14S11), which is marked with a large metal sign that reads, "Big Meadow." Turn east and drive 3.8 miles to Big Meadow campground. There's a small parking area on the south side of the road, directly across from the guard station.

The trailhead is marked by a brown fiberglass post. As you begin hiking south, watch closely, because the trail is difficult to follow as it passes through the campground.

At the south end of the campground, the trail cross Big Meadow Creek, then turns more to the east and begins climbing through lodgepole pines, red firs, and Jeffrey pines.

By about 3/4 miles, you cross a small creek lush with ferns.

You now begin having some good views of the Monarch Divide, to the north.

At 1 1/2 miles, and an elevation of about 8,000 feet, after passing through an area that has been logged, you come to Fox Meadow, where there is a small wooden sign and a trail register.

By 2 miles, and an elevation of 8200 feet, you come to a trail junction marked by a wooden sign. The trail to Jennie Lake turns to the south, uphill.

The trail now climbs steeply through a dense forest of red firs, and by 2 1/4 miles you come to a sign marking the boundary of the Jennie Lakes Wilderness.

You cross a long stringer meadow, which is the lower end of Poison Meadow, and continue uphill, following near the edge of the long and attractive meadow. The plant which gave the meadow it's ominous-sounding name could be larkspur, lupine, or death camas, all of which contain poisonous alkaloids, and will kill cattle and sheep if eaten in sufficient quantities.

By 3 1/4 miles you begin having some views to the west, of Big Baldy, the North Fork of the Kaweah, and on a clear day, the San Joaquin Valley. On the east slope of Big Baldy you can see large areas of the forest that have been clearcut.

Along the trail here you see the fairly uncommon pinemat manzanita, which grows only about a foot high, yet in some places completely blankets the forest floor.

Besides red firs, you now also see lodgepole pines, as well as a great number of handsome, western white pines, a five-needle pine which has a shape similar to a sugarpine.

As the trail contours around the south side of Shell Mountain, you begin to have views to the east. The low point on the ridge to the distant east is Poop Out Pass, the highest point on this trail.

Trees become much more sparse now, as you pass through a region of large, white, granite slabs. Just below the pass you come to the Stony Creek Trail, described in the chapter of that name, and which leads to Stony Creek Campground.

At 5 miles you reach Poop Out Pass, elevation 9150 feet.

The trail immediately begins descending into the steep Boulder Creek drainage, and you soon have good views of the Monarch Divide, far to the north.

To avoid a large area of exfoliated granite, the trail drops steeply, and then begins contouring around the side of the mountain. Looking to the northeast, you can see a large basin which is the location of Rowell Meadow. The timbered mountain above it is Mitchell Peak, which at 10,365 feet is the highest point in the Jennie Lakes Wilderness.

The trail dips and rises only slightly, until at 7 miles, elevation 9140 feet, you arrive at Jennie Lake, named by rancher Sam Ellis for his wife. The sight of the lake's deep green water, with a backdrop of white granite cliffs, is one of the finest sights in this wilderness area, and gives the impression of being much deeper into the backcountry than you actually are. There are several camp sites around the lake where you can rest.

For those hikers who haven't had enough exercise yet, the trail continues to JO Pass:

From the lake, backtrack down the trail about 200 feet, where you pass through a large fallen red fir which has been bucked out of the trail; from this point, looking to the east, you can now see the trail as it crosses the outlet from the lake. There is no sign marking this junction.

The trail climbs steeply through lodgepoles and red firs. At about 1/2 mile from Jennie Lake, you reach the ridge top, which serves as the boundary between the Jennie Lakes Wilderness and Sequoia National Park.

The trail now turns east and follows the ridge, dipping and rising moderately.

At about 1 1/2 miles from Jennie Lake, you arrive at JO Pass, elevation 9415 feet. The pass (pronounced "jay-oh") acquired its unusual name when an early traveler, John Warren, carved the first two initials of his name on a tree here as a signal to his brother, who was following him.

From this point you can return to Big Meadow by the route you came (distance 8 1/2 miles from this point). Or, you can turn north, descend from JO Pass and follow the Boulder Creek Trail to Big Meadow (distance 10 1/2 miles). Or, with some previous planning, you could turn south and hike to Lodgepole (distance 7 miles), where you would have a vehicle waiting for you.

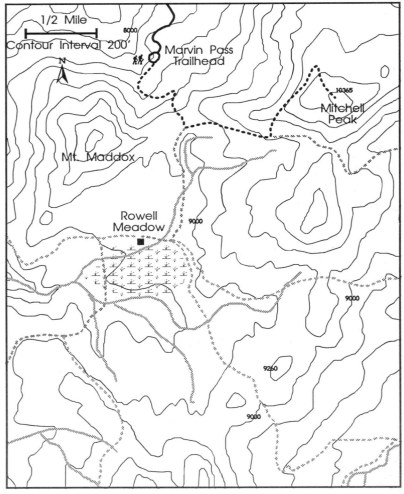

Mitchell Peak Trail

MITCHELL PEAK TRAIL

DISTANCE: 2 3/4 Miles
HIKING TIME: 3 Hours
STARTING ELEVATION: 8400´
HIGHEST ELEVATION: 10365´
DIFFICULTY: Strenuous
USGS MAP: Triple Divide

This trail leads to the highest point in Jennie Lakes Wilderness, and offers the finest view of any day hike in the Kings Canyon area. It's rated here as strenuous because of the 2,000-foot elevation gain, but the distance is so short that most hikers will find it within their ability if they go slowly enough.

The Mitchell Peak Trail begins at the Marvin Pass Trailhead. On the Generals Highway, drive south 6.9 miles from the Grant Grove Visitor Center, or north 4.8 miles from Stony Creek. This brings you to the Big Meadow turnoff (forest service road 14S11). Turn east and drive 10.4 miles to Horse Corral Meadow, where you find a dirt road (13S12), and a small sign pointing south to Marvin Pass. Turn south and drive 2.8 miles to the Marvin Pass Trailhead. Look for the trailhead at the south end of the parking area, where there is also a trail register.

The trail begins by climbing steeply through a partially-logged forest of red firs. In less than 1/4 mile you can see the low point on the ridge ahead, which is Marvin Pass.

At 1 mile, elevation 9040 feet, you reach Marvin Pass, as well as the boundary of Jennie Lakes Wilderness. At the trail junction, turn east, following the trail sign toward Roaring River.

After climbing fairly steeply, at 1 3/4 miles, elevation 9440 feet, you come to another trail junction. Follow the sign pointing to the north, toward Mitchell Peak.

After contouring around to the north side of the peak, the trail levels off a bit. You begin to see foxtail pines, and a few western white pines.

Shortly before reaching the summit, you come to the boundary of Kings Canyon National Park, marked by white signs nailed to the trees.

About 100 yards below the summit, the trail more or less disappears, and you have to scramble over the boulders.

And at 3 miles, elevation 10,365 feet, you reach the summit of Mitchell Peak. To the east, and just below you, you can see Williams Meadow and Sugarloaf Dome. To the distant east, you can see a long stretch of the Great Western Divide. To the south, you can see the Silliman Crest.

At one time there was a fire lookout tower on Mitchell Peak, and you can still see part of the concrete foundation.

Keep in mind that there is the threat of lightning on Mitchell Peak. If the sky is cloudy, or if you can see lightning or feel electricity in the air, descend to a lower elevation.

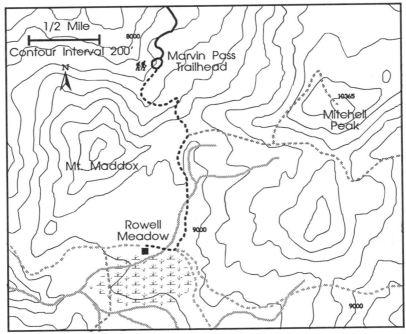

Marvin Pass to Rowell Meadow

MARVIN PASS to ROWELL MEADOW

DISTANCE: 2 Miles

HIKING TIME: 1 1/2 Hours

STARTING ELEVATION: 8400´

HIGHEST ELEVATION: 9040´ at Marvin Pass

DIFFICULTY: Easy

USGS MAP: Triple Divide

Meadows are always popular hiking destinations. Not only are they beautiful to look at, but they're also a good place to spot wildlife. Rowell Meadow is by far the largest Meadow in the Jennie Lakes Wilderness, and though some hikers might find that it is too heavily grazed by cattle to be called pristine, it's still a peaceful place to spend a few hours.

There are several ways to reach Rowell Meadow, and Marvin Pass is one of the easiest. (Also see the Sunset Meadow to Rowell Meadow trail described in this guidebook.)

The trail begins at the Marvin Pass Trailhead. On the Generals Highway, drive south 6.9 miles from the Grant Grove Visitor Center, or north 4.8 miles from Stony Creek. This brings you to the Big Meadow turnoff (forest service road 14S11). Turn east and drive 10.4 miles to Horse Corral Meadow; the road forks several times, but it is well marked. At Horse Corral Meadow, you turn south on Road 13S12 and proceed up the mountain 2.8 miles to the Marvin Pass Trailhead. Look for the trailhead sign at the south end of the parking area, where there is also a trail register.

The trail begins by climbing steeply through a partially logged forest of red firs. In less than 1/4 mile, you can see the low point on the ridge ahead, which is Marvin Pass.

At 1 mile, elevation 9040 feet, you reach Marvin Pass, named by rancher Sam Ellis after his son Marvin. The pass also marks the boundary of Jennie Lakes Wilderness. At the trail junction, follow the sign pointing south to Rowell Meadow.

The trail now descends through a dense forest of lodgepole pines, passing near the edge of a stringer meadow. At 1 3/4 miles, you cross Rowell Meadow Creek.

And at 2 miles, elevation 8850 feet, you come to a trail junction near the edge of Rowell Meadow, named after George and Chester Rowell, who ran sheep here years ago. There are campsites along Rowell Meadow Creek, just a few hundred feet to the west. A patrol cabin, used by the California Department of Water Resources for taking snow surveys, is about 1/4 mile to the west.

From this trail junction, there are several directions a day hiker might explore. Three of them, Pond Meadow, Seville Lake, and JO Pass are described in this guidebook.

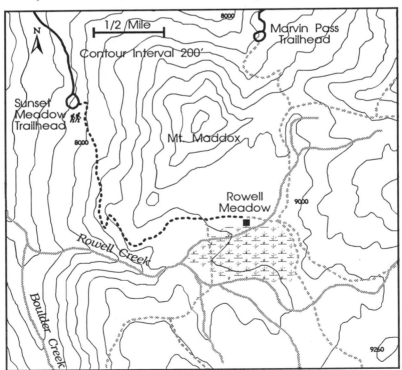

Sunset   Meadow   to   Rowell   Meadow

SUNSET MEADOW to ROWELL MEADOW

DISTANCE: 2 Miles
HIKING TIME: 1 Hour
STARTING ELEVATION: 8000′
HIGHEST ELEVATION: 8850′
DIFFICULTY: Easy
USGS MAP: Giant Forest and Triple Divide

There are several ways to get to Rowell Meadow, some difficult, some easy. This is the easiest and fastest route of all.

To reach the Rowell Meadow Trailhead, drive south on the Generals Highway 6.9 miles from the Grant Grove Visitor Center, or drive north on he Generals Highway 4.8 miles from Stony Creek. This brings you to the Big Meadow turnoff (forest service road 14S11). Turn east, reset your odometer, and drive 9.1 miles on the paved road. Here you reach road 13S14, marked by a large brown sign. Turn south and drive up the dirt road 2.0 miles, where you come to a large parking area just above Sunset Meadow. The trailhead, marked by a bulletin board and register, is on the east side of the parking area.

The trail begins climbing through a logged area of red fir and white fir. At less than 1/4 mile you join the well-worn trail from the Horse Corral Pack Station.

By 1/2 mile, looking to the south, you begin having some views into upper Boulder Creek, which flows from Jennie Lake, and which is the major drainage in the Jennie Lakes Wilderness.

As the trail turns in a more easterly direction, you begin to see a few ponderosa pines and junipers. The rocky drainage flowing from the east is Rowell Meadow Creek.

At 1 mile, elevation 8700 feet, you come to a wooden sign marking the entrance to the Jennie Lakes Wilderness.

By 1 1/2 miles you begin to see, through the lodgepole pines, fingers of lower Rowell Meadow.

At about 1 3/4 miles you come to the junction of the JO Pass Trail, (not shown on the USGS map) which turns to the south.

Continuing to the east, at 2 miles, elevation 8850 feet, you arrive at Rowell Meadow, named after George and Chester Rowell, who ran sheep here years ago. On the south side of the trail is a log cabin used by the California Department of Water Resources for winter snow surveys. The meadow itself is large and attractive, though heavily grazed.

Besides being a pleasant destination for a short hike, Rowell Meadow can almost be considered a trailhead in itself, since there are a total of five trails leading from it. You've already hiked one of them; the other four, Marvin Pass Trail, Pond Meadow Trail, Seville Lake Trail, and JO Pass Trail are described elsewhere in this guidebook.

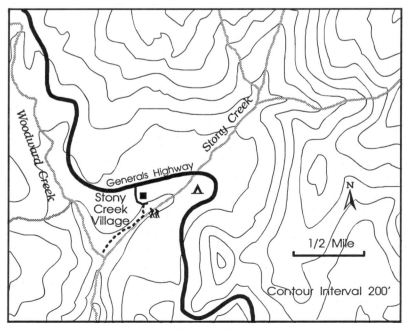

Stony   Creek   Footpath

STONY CREEK FOOTPATH

To Woodward Creek

DISTANCE: 1 Mile
HIKING TIME: 30 Minutes
STARTING ELEVATION: 6400´
LOWEST ELEVATION: 6200´
DIFFICULTY: Moderate
USGS MAP: Giant Forest

This short, unmaintained footpath really isn't inside the boundaries of nearby Jennie Lakes Wilderness. But maybe it should be.

This footpath is only for experienced hikers who feel comfortable on unmarked, unmaintained trails. Be extremely careful along the steep and slippery banks of Stony Creek and Woodward Creek, particularly in the spring and early summer when the water level is high. This trail is not suitable for children.

From the parking area at Stony Creek Village, directly across from the market, follow the dirt path that descends in a southeasterly direction about 300 yards to Stony Creek. (If you're staying at Stony Creek Campground, and the creek is low enough to cross safely, simply cross to the west side of the creek, as if you were walking to the market.)

The well-worn footpath follows the west bank of Stony Creek, meandering downstream through the willows and pines. At times the path splits into two paths, and here and there you have to scramble over fallen trees.

After about 1/4 mile you pass a small, lush meadow on the west side of the path.

Before 1/2 mile, the banks of Stony Creek narrow into a rocky gorge. There are several beautiful pools here, but resist their temptation, and follow the footpath as it climbs into the trees to the west. Do not try to follow Stony Creek here!

The view down canyon opens up now, and you can see for about a mile down Stony Creek. The path passes through white firs, ponderosa pines, and manzanita. A sharp eye is necessary in some places to follow the faint path.

At 1 mile, the trail begins descending to Woodward Creek, elevation 6200 feet. The confluence of Woodward and Stony Creeks is too rocky, steep, and slippery for safe travel, but if you turn up Woodward Creek just 200 feet, where the banks are less steep, you find several beautiful pools.

Use extreme caution in this area!

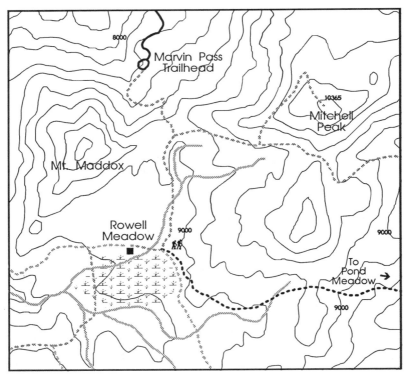

Pond   Meadow   Trail

POND MEADOW TRAIL

From Rowell Meadow

DISTANCE: 2 Miles from Rowell Meadow to the
   Park Boundary

HIKING TIME: 1 Hour

STARTING ELEVATION: 8850´ at Rowell
Meadow

HIGHEST ELEVATION: 9200´ at the Park
   Boundary

DIFFICULTY: Moderate

USGS MAP: Triple Divide

This description begins at the cabin at Rowell Meadow. To reach Rowell Meadow, see either the Marvin Pass or Sunset Meadow chapters of this guidebook.

From the cabin at Rowell Meadow, hike east 1/4 mile to Rowell Meadow Creek, where you see several large, old camps. Continuing beyond the creek just a few hundred yards, you come to a four-way junction marked by a couple of wooden signs. The trail to Pond Meadow and the park service boundary continues to the east.

As you leave Rowell Meadow, the trail begins climbing steeply through lodgepole pines and red firs.

After about 3/4 miles, elevation 9050 feet, the trail crosses a knoll, and then levels off considerably.

At 1 1/4 miles, you cross another of the many forks of Rowell Meadow Creek. Below the trail you see a long, unnamed meadow.

At 1 3/4 miles, elevation 9200 feet, you reach the boundary of Kings Canyon National Park, marked by a metal sign. This is known as the Pond Meadow entrance, although Pond Meadow is still about 1 1/2 miles to the east. (Note that on the USGS Triple Divide Peak quadrangle, the location of Pond Meadow is shown incorrectly.)

Continuing to the east, and descending slightly, at 2 miles you come to a long stringer meadow on the south side of the trail. If you spend a few minutes walking around this area, you are likely to find obsidian flakes and pottery shards—evidence that this trail was used by the Monache Indians as a major route into the Roaring River area. Though the elevation at Roaring River is too high for winter residence, in summer the Indians found an ideal retreat there, plentiful in black-oak acorns, berries, fish and game. By continuing over what is now called Colby Pass, the Monaches could trade with their cousins, the Tubatulabal, who inhabited the Kern River area.

The easiest route back to Rowell Meadow is the same way you came. But experienced, cross-country hikers might enjoy the following alternate route: From the park boundary signs on the Pond Meadow Trail, turn south, following the fir-covered ridge top. The ridge represents the park boundary, and is marked every few hundred feet by white signs nailed to trees about head high. The route rises and falls moderately, but is mostly clear of brush. After following the ridge for about 3/4 miles, you can obtain a view of the Roaring River country by climbing the knoll marked 9260 feet on the map. Continue following the ridge top until, at 1 mile from the Pond Meadow Trail, elevation 9100 feet, you meet the Seville Lake Trail on a broad saddle. A wooden sign there marks the boundary between the Jennie Lakes Wilderness and Kings Canyon National Park. Turn west and follow the trail 2 miles back to Rowell Meadow.

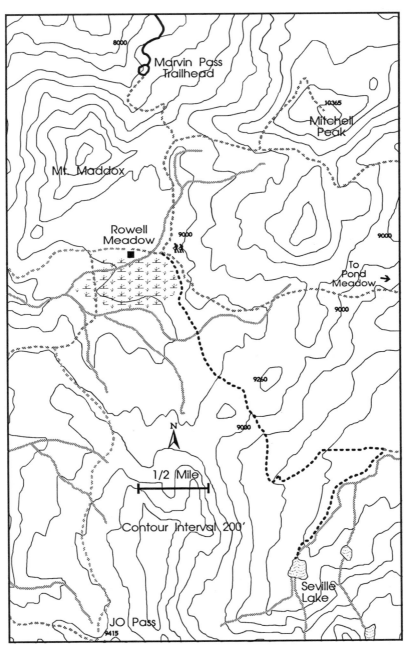

Seville Lake Trail

SEVILLE LAKE TRAIL

From Rowell Meadow

DISTANCE: 4 1/2 miles

HIKING TIME: 2 1/2 Hours

STARTING ELEVATION: 8850´ at Rowell Meadow

HIGHEST ELEVATION: 9100´ at the Park Boundary

LOWEST ELEVATION: 8425´ at Seville Lake

DIFFICULTY: Strenuous

USGS MAP: Triple Divide

Seville Lake is probably beyond the range of most day hikers. (In addition to the 4 1/2 miles from Rowell Meadow, you have to hike 2 miles from either the Marvin Pass trailhead or the Sunset Meadow trailhead; so the round trip hike from the trailhead to Seville Lake, and back to the trailhead, is 13 miles.) But the lake is so pretty, and the hike so pleasing, it's included here for those fit and speedy hikers who want to give it a try.

This trail description begins at Rowell Meadow. To reach Rowell Meadow, see either the Marvin Pass or Sunset Meadow chapters of this guidebook.

From the cabin at Rowell Meadow, hike east 1/4 mile to Rowell Meadow Creek, where you see several large camps beside the trail. Continuing beyond the creek just a few hundred yards, you come to a four-way junction marked by a couple of wooden signs. The Seville Lake Trail turns south, skirting the edge of Rowell Meadow.

The trail then climbs gently, passing several small meadows nearly overgrown with lodgepoles. At about 1 mile from

Rowell Meadow, you cross one of the many forks of Rowell Meadow Creek.

At 2 miles, elevation 9100 feet, you reach the boundary of Kings Canyon National Park, in a broad saddle covered with large red firs. The boundary is marked with a pair of trail signs. The trail now descends rather steeply, passing through a dense forest of lodgepoles and firs. Distant views are scarce here, but looking to the south you may have an occasional view of craggy Kettle Peak, which rises almost directly above Seville Lake.

At 3 1/2 miles, elevation 8250 feet, you come to a trail junction in a dense thicket of young lodgepole pines. Seville Lake is to the south.

The trail climbs very gently, following a stringer meadow along the lake's outlet. Dodecatheons, or shooting stars, are abundant here; their starchy roots are edible if roasted. If you're lucky enough to get here before the birds, you might get to taste one of the wild strawberries growing along the trail.

And at 4 1/2 miles, elevation 8425 feet, you reach Seville Lake, which at one time was known as Sheep Camp Lake. With its rugged backdrop of the Silliman Crest, peaceful Seville Lake is as lovely as any lake in the southern Sierra, and the perfect place to lounge away an afternoon.

Don't forget that the return hike will take you perhaps an hour longer because you are starting about 500 feet lower.

One final note: After studying a topographic map, experienced cross-country hikers will see an obvious shortcut which can eliminate the last one mile of the route to Seville Lake. That shortcut won't be described here, except to say that it is perfectly passable, though the dense lodgepole thickets make the route rougher than one might like.

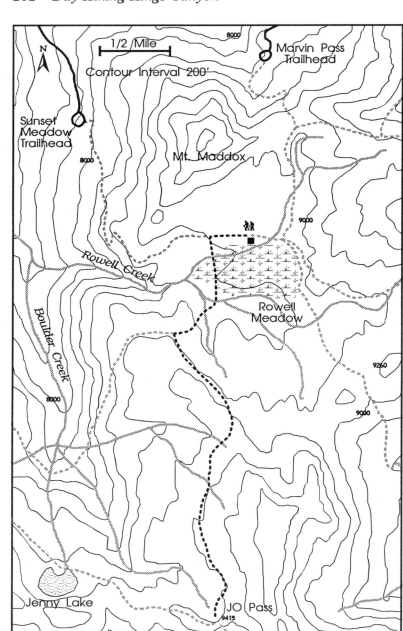

JO Pass Trail

JO PASS TRAIL

From Rowell Meadow

DISTANCE: 4 Miles

HIKING TIME: 2 Hours

STARTING ELEVATION: 8850′ at Rowell Meadow

HIGHEST ELEVATION: 9415′ at JO Pass

DIFFICULTY: Moderate

USGS MAP: Triple Divide

Most hikers would consider a trip to JO Pass a pleasant day's excursion all by itself. But many hikers overlook the fact that you can use this route as a back door to Jennie Lake. If you can arrange the transportation, you can see a considerable portion of the Jennie Lakes Wilderness in one day by hiking from Sunset Meadow, to Rowell Meadow, to JO Pass, to Jennie Lake, to Big Meadow.

This trail description begins at Rowell Meadow. To reach Rowell Meadow, see either the Marvin Pass or Sunset Meadow chapters of this guidebook.

The JO Pass trailhead is about 1/4 mile west of the cabin at Rowell Meadow, on the trail between Sunset Meadow and Rowell Meadow, and is marked by a wooden sign.

The trail leads due south, passing through lodgepole pines, and descending slightly as it crosses the lower end of Rowell Meadow. It crosses a fork of Rowell Meadow Creek, then follows a meandering route, dipping and rising.

At 1/2 mile you cross another fork of Rowell Meadow Creek, followed in a few hundred feet by yet another. Here the trail begins climbing more steeply as it turns gradually to the west. Looking to the northeast, you can see Mitchell Peak, and almost due north, Mt. Maddox.

At about 1 mile, elevation 9,000 feet, you come to the junction of the Weaver Lake Trail. The trail to JO Pass continues to the south, climbing moderately through a forest of red firs, lodgepoles, and western white pines.

At about 2 miles you reach the top of a broad, flat, sandy ridge, known as Profile View, elevation 9300 feet.

The trail now traverses up the side of the ridge, crossing several small creeks which may be dry late in the year. By 3 miles, looking back to the north, you have some good views of Spanish Mountain.

At 3 1/2 miles, and an elevation of about 9450 feet, the trail levels off, and even descends slightly, as you follow above a long stringer meadow.

And at 4 miles you arrive at JO Pass, elevation 9415 feet. The pass (pronounced "jay-oh") acquired its unusual name when an early traveler, John Warren, carved the first two initials of his name on a tree here as a signal to his brother, who was following him. Apparently, that tree is no longer standing, though you might enjoy spending a few minutes looking for it.

From this point you have several options: You can return to Rowell Meadow by the route you came. You can turn west and descend to Jennie Lake (1 1/2 miles) and to Big Meadow (8 1/2 miles). Or, with some previous planning, you can turn south and hike to Lodgepole (distance 7 miles), where you would have a vehicle waiting for you.

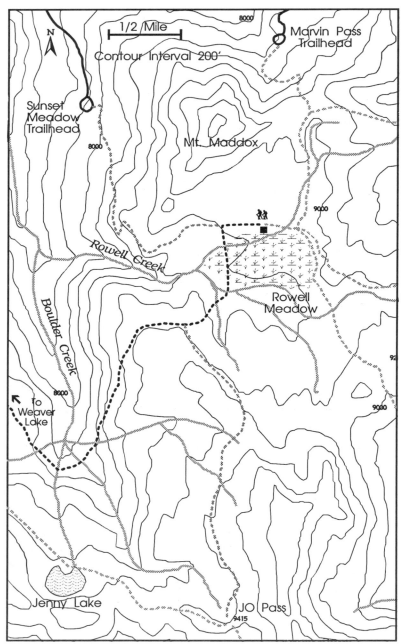

Boulder Creek Trail

BOULDER CREEK TRAIL

Rowell Meadow to Weaver Lake to Big Meadow

DISTANCE: 6 Miles to Weaver Lake; 8 1/2 Miles
to Big Meadow

HIKING TIME: 3 Hours to Weaver Lake; 4 Hours
to Big Meadow

STARTING ELEVATION: 8850′ at Rowell
Meadow

LOWEST ELEVATION: 8300′ at Boulder Creek;
7600' at Big Meadow

HIGHEST ELEVATION: 9000′

DIFFICULTY: Strenuous

USGS MAPS: Triple Divide and Giant Forest

This trail doesn't get used much, and that's good for those
hikers who like to get lost for a day. It's the only trail that gives
access to the rugged and beautiful upper Boulder Creek, which
is the main artery of the Jennie Lakes Wilderness, and this trail
also provides a backdoor route to Weaver Lake.

This trail description begins at Rowell Meadow. To reach
Rowell Meadow, see either the Marvin Pass or Sunset Meadow
chapters of this guidebook.

To hike this trail the way it's described here, as a one-way
trail, you must have somebody drop you off at Sunset Meadow
and pick you up at Big Meadow, or arrange transportation in
some other way.

Begin hiking at the JO Pass trailhead, which is about 1/4
mile west of the cabin at Rowell Meadow, on the trail between

Sunset Meadow and Rowell Meadow. That junction is marked by a wooden sign.

The trail heads due south, passing through lodgepole pines, and descending slightly as it crosses the lower end of Rowell Meadow. It crosses a fork of Rowell Meadow Creek, then follows a meandering route, dipping and rising.

At 1/2 mile you cross another fork of Rowell Meadow Creek, followed in a few hundred feet by yet another. Here the trail begins climbing more steeply, as it turns gradually to the west. Looking to the northeast, you can see Mitchell Peak, and almost due north, Mt. Maddox.

At about 1 mile, elevation 9,000 feet, you come to the junction of the JO Pass Trail, marked by a wooden sign; the trail to Boulder Creek and Weaver Lake turns to the west.

After contouring around the ridge, through a forest of red firs and western white pines, the trail begins descending steeply to Boulder Creek, which you can see several hundred feet below. On this warm southwest-facing slope, the red firs are almost completely replaced by ponderosa pines and manzanita.

Looking across the canyon to the west, you can see the ridge you must climb to reach Weaver Lake. And looking to the south, you can see the approximate location of Jennie Lake, just below the pyramid-shaped peak.

At about 3 miles, elevation 8300 feet, you reach the bottom of the canyon, which is thick with red willows, azaleas, thimbleberries, and ferns. Here the trail crosses several forks of Boulder Creek within the next 1/4 mile. The main fork has its source at Jennie Lake, and during the spring runoff it is a rushing torrent. Surprisingly, though, late in the year all the forks of Boulder Creek combined don't carry much water. Even though the Boulder Creek watershed is fairly large, it isn't high enough to preserve a large snow pack late into the summer.

There are several small camps in the canyon bottom where you can rest, or while away a peaceful day.

The trail now begins climbing steeply up the west side of the canyon, which again is dominated by red firs. When it first appears as if you have reached the top of the ridge, you still have another 1/4 mile or so to climb. Through the trees you have some good views of the Monarch Divide, to the north.

You finally reach the top of the ridge at about 4 1/2 miles, elevation 8800 feet, and soon pass by a large, unnamed meadow below the trail. If you approach the meadow quietly, you may see a deer or bear.

The trail now follows a rather meandering route, as if it can't decide where it's going.

At about 5 1/2 miles, you meet the well-worn Weaver Lake Trail. (Note that on the USGS map, the junction is not shown at the correct location.) Though this junction is not marked by a trail sign, at the time of this writing an old wooden post was standing at the junction. To reach Weaver Lake, you turn south and climb gently for less than 1/2 mile.

To continue on to Big Meadow, turn to the northwest at the junction. You soon cross a stringer meadow along Weaver Creek, which is likely to be dry late in the year.

The trail descends through a forest of red firs, and at about 6 1/4 miles you reach the boundary of the Jennie Lakes Wilderness, marked by a wooden sign.

At 6 1/2 miles, elevation 8200 feet, you come to a small creek which is likely to be flowing even late in the year. Just past this creek you can see the junction of the Jennie Lake Trail.

7 miles, elevation 8,000 feet, brings you to Fox Meadow, marked by a wooden sign and a trail register.

You now climb briefly, passing through a logged area, then begin your final descent to Big Meadow, 8 1/2 miles, elevation 7600 feet.

After you cross Big Meadow Creek, you are in the campground. To reach the parking area on the Big Meadow Road, continue north 1/4 mile, following the trail markers through the campground.

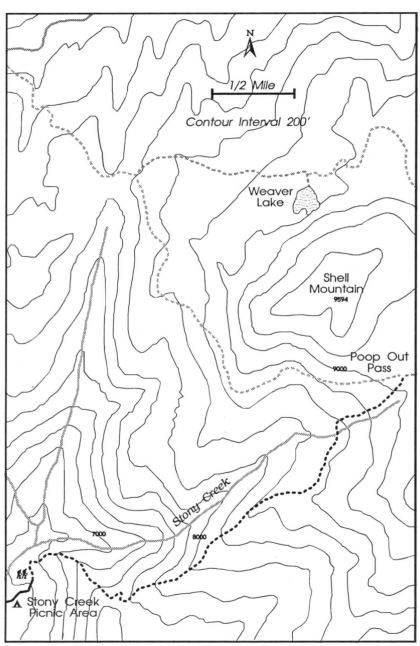

Stony Creek Trail

STONY CREEK TRAIL

To Poop Out Pass and Jennie Lake

DISTANCE: 4 miles
HIKING TIME: 3 Hours
STARTING ELEVATION: 6500´
HIGHEST ELEVATION: 9150´
DIFFICULTY: Strenuous
USGS MAP: Giant Forest

Although this trail will lead you to Jennie Lake, you can get to Jennie Lake easier, and save about 1,000 feet of climbing, by beginning at Big Meadows. The real value of this trail, at least for the day hiker, is that it provides access to upper Stony Creek, in a corner of the Jennie Lakes Wilderness where not too many people go.

The Stony Creek Trail begins at the Stony Creek Picnic Area. From Stony Creek Village, drive or walk 0.5 miles east on the Generals Highway. A wooden sign marks the entrance to the picnic area on the north side of the highway; turn into the picnic area and proceed 0.3 miles to the small parking area at the north end.

The trailhead is about 200 feet to the east (or to your right as you enter the parking area). A brown fiberglass post marks the trail.

Because of the south-facing slope, this trail can be warm in the summer, so plan for an early start. It's also a dry trail during much of the year, so be sure to carry water.

About 1/8 mile up the trail, you come to a trail sign, and shortly beyond that a trail register. It's a good idea to sign this register; not only does it let the Forest Service know that people are using their wilderness trails, but, in the unlikely case of an accident, it provides a record of your hiking plans.

The trail climbs steeply through a very diverse forest of Jeffrey pines, cedars, white firs, white pines, and sugarpines. Some of this area has been logged.

After about 1/2 mile, at an elevation of about 6800 feet, you reach the boundary of the 10,500-acre Jennie Lakes Wilderness. No logging has been allowed beyond this point, but looking back to the west, toward Big Baldy, you can see large areas in Sequoia National Forest that have been clearcut.

At about 1 mile, elevation 7600 feet, you gain the ridge top which marks the boundary with Sequoia National Park. The trail now follows that ridge.

At about 8,000 feet you reach an open rocky area with just a scattering of Jeffrey Pines. Here you begin to have views of peaks on the Great Western Divide, to the east.

The trail continues to climb steeply, until about 3 miles, elevation 8500 feet, where it levels off considerably.

The trail now contours gradually in a more northerly direction, and at 3 1/2 miles you reach the west fork of Stony Creek, where you will likely find water even late in the summer. This small creek (too small for fishing), makes a fine destination for the day, and a good place to rest before heading back. For those hikers who wish to continue hiking, though, the description to Jennie Lake is as follows:

From the Stony Creek crossing, the trail climbs steeply through a forest of red firs, until at about 9050 feet you reach the junction of the Jennie Lake Trail, marked by a wooden trail sign. The trail to the west descends to Big Meadow, while the trail to the east climbs to the well-named Poop Out Pass, elevation 9150 feet, distance 4 miles.

Continuing on to Jennie Lake, the trail immediately begins descending into the steep Boulder Creek drainage, and you soon have good views of the Monarch Divide, far to the north.

To avoid a large area of exfoliated granite, the trail drops steeply, and then begins contouring around the side of the mountain. Looking to the northeast, you can see a large basin which is the location of Rowell Meadow. The timbered mountain above it is Mitchell Peak, which at 10,365 feet is the highest point in the Jennie Lakes Wilderness.

The trail dips and rises only slightly, until at 6 miles, elevation 9140 feet, you arrive at Jennie Lake.

A final suggestion: If you're staying at Stony Creek campground, and you're looking for a full day's activity, have someone drive you to Big Meadow; hike to Jennie Lake, backtrack to Poop Out Pass, then hike down the Stony Creek Trail to Stony Creek Campground—total mileage about 13 miles.

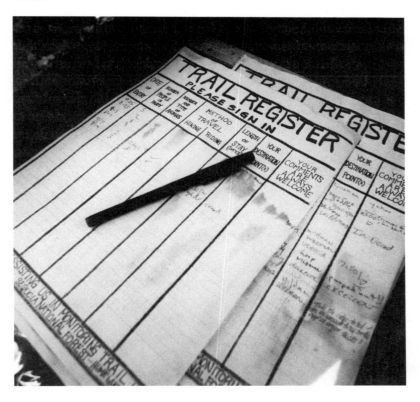

Index

To Order:

Day Hiking Kings Canyon

or

Day Hiking Sequoia

Please send $14.00 check or money order, to:

Manzanita Press
PO Box 720
Three Rivers, CA 93271

This price includes tax, postage, and handling.
Your order will be shipped within three days after it is received.

Wholesalers and distributors, please write to the same address, or call Manzanita Press at 209-561-4666, for our discount schedule.

About the Author

Steve Sorensen worked in the resources management division at Sequoia and Kings Canyon National Parks for fourteen years, followed by several years as a journalist. He now works as a writer, and lives in Three Rivers, California, just outside of Sequoia and Kings Canyon National Parks, with his wife and two sons.